No Greater Work
Meditations on Church Documents for Educators

PASTORAL TEXTS AND RESOURCES DIVISION

Alliance for Catholic Education Press
at the University of Notre Dame

No Greater Work
Meditations on Church Documents for Educators

Edited by
James M. Frabutt
Anthony C. Holter
Ronald J. Nuzzi

ALLIANCE FOR CATHOLIC EDUCATION PRESS
AT THE UNIVERSITY OF NOTRE DAME

NOTRE DAME, INDIANA

Alliance for Catholic Education Press
University of Notre Dame
158 IEI Building
Notre Dame, IN 46556
http://acepress.nd.edu

ISBN: 978-1-935788-01-0

Cover and interior graphics designed by Mary Jo Adams Kocovski
Interior layout by Julie Wernick Dallavis

Library of Congress Cataloging-in-Publication Data

No greater work : meditations on church documents for educators / edited
by James M. Frabutt, Anthony C. Holter, Ronald J. Nuzzi.
    p. cm.
  Summary: "A prayer resource for educators and administrators in Catholic
schools that offers responses to quotations from Church documents in
the forms of reflective narratives, contemplative questions, and original
prayers"--Provided by publisher.
  Includes bibliographical references and indexes.
  ISBN 978-1-935788-01-0 (pbk. : alk. paper)
  1. Catholic teachers--Prayers and devotions. 2. School administrators-
-Prayers and devotions. 3. Catholic Church--Education--Meditations. I.
Frabutt, James M., 1972- II. Holter, Anthony C., 1977- III. Nuzzi, Ronald
James, 1958-
  BX2170.T43N6 2010
  242'.88--dc22
                          2010031427

This book was printed on acid-free paper.

Printed in the United States of America.

Table of Contents

Acknowledgments   *vii*

Preface   *ix*

Documents   *xi*

Daily Reflections   1

References   183

Document Index   185

Contributor Index   187

About the Contributors   189

Acknowledgments

All members of the Body of Christ—parents, teachers, school leaders, family, friends, and community—bear the duty of educating the young. We believe that there is no greater work than accepting this sacred duty. While carried forth now by modern-day evangelists, the Church has celebrated for centuries the apostolic mission of Catholic education, a fact foregrounded and celebrated in this text.

We acknowledge and thank Brother William Dygert, C.S.C., for his initial suggestion to compile excerpts from the many Church documents that expressly address the mission of Catholic schools. Brother William has decades of experience as a Catholic educational leader, and currently serves as Superintendent of Schools in the Diocese of Peoria and as an instructor in the Mary Ann Remick Leadership Program at the University of Notre Dame.

We are grateful to the school teachers and leaders, many of them graduates of the Remick Leadership Program, whose lived experiences in Catholic schools permeate these pages. Their heartfelt reflections and prayers are testament to a vocation that brings life and sustenance to others, especially students.

We are edified by the young voices—university undergraduates and novice teachers—whose contributions offer a fortifying glimpse into the lived present and hoped for future of our Church.

Many friends, colleagues, and benefactors stand behind this work and have helped in ways known and unknown to advance the mission of Catholic education. They are too numerous to mention here, yet we remain ever grateful for their life-giving support. Among our most vivacious advocates are the Reverend Timothy R. Scully, C.S.C., founder of the Alliance for Catholic Education, the Goizueta Foundation, and Mary Ann and Jack Remick. Our skilled colleagues, Mary Jo Adams-Kocovski and Julie Dallavis, invested much time and energy in shaping our vision into something that will bless Catholic education at every level. But it is to our students that we owe our deepest gratitude, for it was their delight in discovering these documents that encouraged us to draw attention anew to their abiding power.

Preface

"With good reason therefore did St. John Chrysostom say, 'What greater work is there than training the mind and forming the habits of the young?'"

The Church has much to say about its Catholic schools, for they emanate from Her very heart. The writings of popes, documents from Vatican offices, statements of Church councils, and the pastoral letters of bishops all contribute to a significant compendium of teaching on the nature and aims of Catholic schools. Taken as a whole, these documents give voice to that which is unique, most distinctive, most cherished, and most Christ-centered about our Catholic schools.

Yet, many Catholic school leaders and teachers are unfamiliar with these seminal touchstones of our faith. These writings are both unknown and unread, leaving a veritable treasure untapped. A core aim of this text is to promote a more intimate engagement with what some have termed one of the Church's "best kept secrets."

This text draws upon twenty-five source documents that together constitute much of the Church's official teaching on Catholic schools and education. Dating from 1885 to as recent as 2007, the original documents were authored by popes, Vatican congregations, ecumenical councils, and episcopal conferences. We selected 180 excerpts from these source documents, which are presented here with a composed prayer, a personal reflection, or a set of contemplation/discussion questions. The material after each excerpt was contributed by Catholic school teachers, leaders, professors, or researchers from across the United States. Their perspective lends the voice of lived experience to each of the excerpts, challenging us all to a deeper engagement with the material.

We invite you to approach the contents of this text as you would a good friend or treasures that you hold dear: take good care and visit often. First, the challenge to care entails a commitment to deeper understanding. Sit with each entry prayerfully. Perhaps meditate on a thought, a reflection, or a challenge that is inherent in each. Try to soak in the wisdom of the tradition. Beyond the initial questions, prayers, and reflections offered here, contemplate your own interpretation and application, considering the unique context not only of your own classroom or school, but your personal spirituality and vocation. Second, be a regular visitor—one who checks in often, gets reacquainted, and never strays too far from these important guiding teachings. Mindful that these writings articulate the distinctive mark of Catholic schools, immerse yourself in them frequently, especially as new challenges arise and you need sustenance for the journey.

Documents

Catechetical Documents

1997	*Catechism of the Catholic Church*

Encyclicals and Other Papal Documents

1885	Leo XIII	*Spectata Fides* [On Christian Education]
1890	Leo XIII	*Sapientiae Christianae* [On Christians as Citizens]
1929	Pius XI	*Divini Ilius Magistri* [On Christian Education]
1961	John XXIII	*Mater et Magistra* [On Christianity and Social Progress]
1975	Paul VI	*Evangelii Nuntiandi* [On Evangelization in the Modern World]
1979	John Paul II	*Catechesi Tradendae* [On Catechesis in Our Time]
1981	John Paul II	*Familiaris Consortio* [The Role of the Christian Family in the Modern World]
1994	John Paul II	*Gratissimam Sane* [Letter to Families]
1999	John Paul II	*Ecclesia in America* [The Church in America]

Documents of the Second Vatican Council

1965	Vatican II	*Gaudium et Spes* [On the Church in the Modern World]
1965	Vatican II	*Gravissimum Educationis* [Declaration on Christian Education]

Documents from the Roman Curia

1977	Sacred Congregation for Catholic Education	*The Catholic School*
1982	Sacred Congregation for Catholic Education	*Lay Catholics in Schools*
1988	Congregation for Catholic Education	*The Religious Dimension of Education in a Catholic School*
1998	Congregation for Catholic Education	*The Catholic School on the Threshold of the Third Millennium*
2002	Congregation for Catholic Education	*Consecrated Persons and Their Mission in Schools*
2004	Pontifical Council for Justice and Peace	*The Compendium of the Social Doctrine of the Church*
2007	Congregation for Catholic Education	*Educating Together in Catholic Schools*

Documents from the United States Bishops

1972	National Conference of Catholic Bishops/ United States Catholic Conference (NCCB/USCC)	*To Teach as Jesus Did*
1976	United States Catholic Conference	*Teach Them!*
1990	NCCB/USCC	*In Support of Catholic Elementary and Secondary Schools*
1995	United States Catholic Conference	*Principles for Educational Reform in the United States*
1999	NCCB/USCC	*Our Hearts Were Burning Within Us*
2005	United States Conference of Catholic Bishops	*Renewing Our Commitment to Catholic Elementary and Secondary Schools in the Third Millennium*

Daily Reflections

"Beautiful indeed and of great importance is the vocation of all those who aid parents in fulfilling their duties and who, as representatives of the human community, undertake the task of education in schools. This vocation demands special qualities of mind and heart, very careful preparation, and continuing readiness to renew and to adapt."

GRAVISSIMUM EDUCATIONIS §5

Catholic school administrators constantly strive to mold and shape their teachers. Through professional development, in-service meetings, and modeling desired behaviors, administrators seek to employ those teachers who not only understand the curriculum, but who carry within them a genuine love for their profession and for the students that they directly impact. Administrators use the school's mission statement, the school's published philosophy, or the charism of the order to ensure a communal attitude toward the work at hand.

In my career, I have been privileged to work with many teachers who were born to instruct. Their persona often changed when they walked to the front of the classroom. Some were extroverts; others were quite introverted in adult conversations. But, in their classroom, they seemed to light up! Their eyes were those of an enthusiastic presenter whose story kept students on the edge of their seats. Their minds embraced the curriculum and meshed it with an internal understanding of child development that simply made the information come alive. Yet, it was their hearts and their genuine love of learning that made them stand ahead of their peers.

One year, the high school faculty embarked upon a study of possible schedule changes. As the principal, I dreaded the meetings that were to come. Yet, because of additional graduation requirements, our current schedule would no longer work. As I approached the faculty, I reminded the teachers that we did not want high school to become a five-year experience for our students. So, faculty members had to be open, examine all options, and collaborate on the best solution. "Why?" was the question some veteran teachers voiced aloud. Many teachers made comments about "reinventing the wheel" or "fixing something that did not seem broken." But it was the teacher with the most seniority, the one who could have led the discussions, who stepped forward and addressed the faculty meeting with a calm voice. His words have resonated in my ears many different times. His statements and his charge were completely unsolicited, but did not really surprise me. His leadership, the ability to step up when others were complaining about additional work, and his passionate words about making the educational process better for our students calmed the negativity, allowed the process to gel, and moved the discussions forward in a positive direction.

Teaching is a vocation. Teaching requires us to challenge our students while we challenge ourselves. Teaching: having the faith that God will provide you with the knowledge, passion, enthusiasm, and love to be a role model for our youth!

ROSANN WHITING

"It must never be forgotten that the purpose of instruction at school is education, that is, the development of man from within, freeing him from that conditioning which would prevent him from becoming a fully integrated human being."

THE CATHOLIC SCHOOL §29

When my heart becomes disconnected from my mind,
    Lord, make me whole.
When my faith is tried by doubt,
    Lord, make me whole.
When my actions fall short of my intentions,
    Lord, make me whole.
When my aspirations are not the equal of my gifts,
    Lord, make me whole.
Until I join the fullness of your Resurrection,
    Lord, make me whole.

JIM FRABUTT

"An organic, critical, and value-oriented communication of culture clearly includes the communication of truth and knowledge; while doing this, a Catholic teacher should always be alert for opportunities to initiate the appropriate dialogue between culture and faith—two things which are intimately related—in order to bring the interior synthesis of the student to this deeper level."

LAY CATHOLICS IN SCHOOLS §29

When I was young, if I was reading in the dark, my mother would always remind me to turn on a light, so I could really see what was on the page and wouldn't ruin my eyes. When I think of the mission of Catholic school education, I am always reminded of this advice, for I view the mission of Catholic schools as teaching and learning in the light of faith, of "turning on," so to speak, the light of faith with regard to the communication of values and culture, of truth and knowledge.

Catholic school education is really about worldview, that is, the eyes through which a person views reality. Knowledge is not neutral. What we come to know, to believe, and to accept as true are largely determined by our attitude, our stance toward life. In technological terms we might say that our stance toward life is our default position and that Catholic school education is all about forming this Catholic default position.

This stance toward life or preset position is the consequence of synthesis, that is, of putting things together. And it is the job of Catholic school educators to help students make these connections, to engage in the dialogue between faith and culture through the light of faith and to transform the culture, not be transformed by it. Catholic school students will become leavens in society to the extent that the Catholic school as a learning community immerses them in a Catholic worldview by all that is said and done both inside and outside the classroom. Or to paraphrase my mother's advice, a Catholic school community needs to be sure to turn on the light of faith so while learning students can see clearly what is really on the page, make the right connections, and learn at a deeper level!

BROTHER WILLIAM DYGERT, C.S.C.

4

"In this way, the educational community makes room for the gifts of the Spirit and acknowledges these diversities as wealth. A genuine ecclesial maturity, nourished by the encounter with Christ in the sacraments, will make it possible to develop 'whether of the more traditional kind or the newer ecclesial movements...a vitality that is God's gift,' for the entire scholastic community and for the educational journey itself."

EDUCATING TOGETHER IN CATHOLIC SCHOOLS §17

Lord,
We thank you for showering us with many gifts, knowing that your spirit brings them alive in us.

Bless our Church
    that she might be a good shepherd to her flock.
Bless our school
    that we might model your love in the world.
Bless our administrators
    that, like the apostles, they might lead others to You.
Bless our teachers
    that they might guide their students to the truth.
Bless our nurses and counselors
    that they might provide a healing touch.
Bless the prophets among us
    who call us back to Your loving embrace when we stray.
Bless those among us
    who speak a different language and remind us to welcome the stranger.
Bless our secretaries, assistants and aids
    who enable us to use our gifts more efficiently and effectively.

In You we see the image of the Invisible God. We are called to be Your image in the world. Give us the courage and compassion to accomplish this each day.
Amen.

SISTER BARBARA KANE, O.P.

5

"The atmosphere and relationships in the school are as much the focus of the Catholic school as is the formal religious education class."

TEACH THEM! §30

The existence of religious education courses does not make a school Catholic. The culture that permeates a Catholic school should be transparently evident as one moves throughout the building. A visitor should feel the presence of grace from the first greeting in the front office to every discourse heard in the classroom, hallway, gymnasium, and cafeteria. It is in these places, sometimes more visibly than in the pews of the chapel or the church, that we find the existence of true relationship with Christ.

Measuring the Catholicity of a school is a subjective business. Ultimately, the best evidence that we are imparting the wisdom of Catholic education cannot be gleaned from a multiple choice or essay test. It is the daily commitment to living the Gospel values that suggests that Christian relationships have formed and are an integral part of the daily lives of our students. As with many aspects of education, it is the ability to apply acquired knowledge and concepts that validates the learning process.

Formal religious education is an important foundation in Catholic schools, but educators who place emphasis only on acquisition of information about our faith miss a critical opportunity to truly fulfill the mission of Catholic education. Knowledge without the desire or ability to apply it is just a cognitive exercise. Providing an educational environment that encourages students to witness to their faith should be the ultimate focus of the school.

The challenge we face as Catholic educators is to find balance between the knowledge of our faith and the living of our faith. Administrators need to communicate this expectation to teachers. A leadership style that promotes positive relationships between faculty members creates a model that demonstrates the importance of relationship building to students. Administrators should provide quality staff development that empowers teachers to build a school with positive Catholic culture.

We have many formal religion curricula from which to choose, but bringing the pages of our religion text alive and making them relevant to our students is the greatest challenge of all.

LORI MOREAU

"The fecundity of conjugal love cannot be reduced solely to the procreation of children, but must extend to their moral education and their spiritual formation. 'The role of parents in education is of such importance that it is almost impossible to provide an adequate substitute.' The right and the duty of parents to educate their children are primordial and inalienable."

CATECHISM OF THE CATHOLIC CHURCH §2221

---

1. What are some of the challenges you face when working collaboratively with parents?

2. Is there a particular parent situation that you are currently dealing with that needs to be resolved or a relationship that you feel needs mending?

3. Brainstorm some ways that you can make the parents of your students feel more supported in their work as primary educators.

4. Think of ways that you can bring God into the collaborative work you do with the parents of your students.

PAMELA LYONS

"Having the mind of the Son means to attend his school daily, to learn from him to have a heart that is meek and humble, courageous and passionate. It means allowing oneself to be educated by Christ, the eternal Word of the Father and, to be drawn to him, the heart and centre of the world, choosing his same form of life."

CONSECRATED PERSONS AND THEIR MISSION IN SCHOOLS §9

Lord, God,
So that my life as a Catholic school educator may be for those that I teach a sign of your saving love, let me put on the mind of Your Son, Christ the teacher.

Grant me a heart that is meek and humble, a will that is courageous and passionate, a disposition that is warm and welcoming, and a mind that is curious and full of wonder.

Fill me with faith and the desire to share it,
knowledge and the talent to impart it,
care and the ability to exercise it,
wisdom and the means to apply it,
hope and the capacity to infuse it,
fidelity and the strength to sustain it.

Let me appreciate that my students must know first that I care before they will come to care about what I know.

Fill me with a love of knowledge and a knowledge of love, and, by your grace, as I teach by word, deed, and example, let me always learn from the words, deeds, and example of those I serve with and of those for whom I serve.

These things I ask in the name of Your Son,
Christ, my teacher.
Amen.

BROTHER WILLIAM DYGERT, C.S.C.

*"It is precisely in the Gospel of Christ, taking root in the minds
and lives of the faithful, that the Catholic school finds its definition."*

THE CATHOLIC SCHOOL §9

In March of 2009, I took a group of ten students from Saint Augustine Catholic High School in Tucson, Arizona, on a service trip
to San Carlos, Arizona. While on the Native American reservation, we
spent time with Apache children at Saint Charles Catholic School.

During the day, some students from Saint Augustine tutored San
Carlos students in reading and writing, while others from our group
helped with rehabilitation projects. In the afternoon, our group spent
time learning about the challenges and hopes of life on the reservation. In the evening, after the students prepared a meal, our group
gathered for prayer and reflection on the day's events. Each group
shared a passage from the Gospel, and related it to an experience
from the day.

On one evening of prayer, toward the end of our time together,
the group began connecting themes from the Gospels to their experiences at San Carlos and their overall time at Saint Augustine. Many
of the students expressed deep joy in being able to experience the
hope and optimism found in living out the Gospel. Another student,
while struggling to find meaning in the suffering the Apache faced,
discerned a connection to the Paschal Mystery.

Above all, the students shared deep gratitude for being able to
live out their faith in actions of service to others. Most importantly,
perhaps, the profound joy and gratitude for their Catholic education
flowed directly from these formative moments of Catholic community, service, and work for social justice. Allowing young Catholics the
opportunity to witness the Gospel to others is indeed a definitive hall-
mark of Catholic schools.

PETER CORRIGAN

"The Catholic school sets out to be a school for the human person and of human persons. 'The person of each individual human being, in his or her material and spiritual needs, is at the heart of Christ's teaching: this is why the promotion of the human person is the goal of the Catholic school.'"

THE CATHOLIC SCHOOL ON THE THRESHOLD OF THE THIRD MILLENNIUM §9

1. What opportunities do students and staff have to affirm and promote human dignity at all stages of life? What special events or activities during the year reify the sanctity of human life at this school?

2. How is the promotion of the human person manifest in the school handbook, discipline policies and procedures, and in classroom instruction and interaction? What changes could be made in any of these areas to affirm that this school is a place of human formation in Christian maturity?

3. Who are the marginalized or outcast students and staff in the school community? Whose voices have been muted, contributions diminished, talents overlooked because of language, socioeconomic factors, or other realities? What can I do as a school leader to ensure their dignity is upheld in and through this school?

ANTHONY HOLTER

"All of this demands that Catholic educators develop in themselves, and cultivate in their students, a keen social awareness and a profound sense of civic and political responsibility. The Catholic educator, in other words, must be committed to the task of forming men and women who will make the 'civilization of love' a reality."

LAY CATHOLICS IN SCHOOLS §19

Loving God,
I ask You today for guidance in all of my work in life, both here at my Catholic school and in all aspects of my daily life. Lead me to a renewed relationship with You, God, so that I may lead my students to the same.

With this, we shall all come to better know Your calling for us in life. I also ask that You lead me to a renewed sense of spirit within my teaching—that I not guide my students to think about a civilization of money and status but instead a civilization of love. For education is a key tool both in fostering a life with You and a life here in this world, and You have called me to take up the role of educator.

Guide me in preparing all of my students so that their future role in society is filled with a sense of social commitment and a dedication to the virtues of the Gospel. May I show through teaching the importance of striving to make a world that is more peaceful and loving. Though we live in a world that has turned away from You, You have not turned away from us; may You guide us all to work toward an appreciation of life and a renewal of the world.

Through faith, hope, and love, may I always be a beacon of light for my students and an example they can turn to as they prepare for their future lives of love with You.
Amen.

KEVIN KIMBERLY

"An adult community whose faith is well-formed and lively will more effectively pass that faith on to the next generation. Moreover, the witness of adults actively continuing their own formation shows children and youth that growth in faith is lifelong and does not end upon reaching adulthood."

OUR HEARTS WERE BURNING WITHIN US §40

---

*M*any Catholic educators have cynically observed that the Sacrament of Confirmation often serves as the ritual marking of teenagers' departure from religious education. This is regrettable. The conviction that faith formation is a lifelong process runs deep in the Catholic tradition, and this teaching is affirmed by insights from fields such as developmental psychology, biology, and pastoral theology. The soul, like the body, changes and develops over time, shedding some elements, while taking on others.

Whenever I was the celebrant for the 6:30 a.m. Sunday Mass at the Church of the Ascension in Kettering, Ohio, during my years at the University of Dayton, I always noticed the loyalty, faithfulness, and predictability of the congregation. Same people, every Sunday, sitting in the same place. I always took the opening procession down the main aisle so we could sing a few verses of the opening hymn, and in good weather, we would go outside before we began rather than walking across the back of the church. Parked in the first row, closest to the church, in the first available spot not reserved for those with disabilities, was always the same car, with the same man, sitting behind the wheel, reading the newspaper. He dutifully drove his wife to Mass every Sunday morning. They came early; she had a series of pre-Mass prayers to say (probably for him). But he never came in. And he was Catholic. I know. I checked. That he would wave to me every time, greet me by name, and smile and show joy to see me just adds to the comic absurdity and spiritual void I still sense recalling the encounters.

One might argue that it could have been worse. Some spouses stay home and do not even bother with the offer to accompany or drive. But I cannot but help to see it as a missed opportunity, a blindness to that grace that is always and everywhere.

FATHER RONALD NUZZI

"The principle that no human act is morally indifferent to one's conscience or before God has clear applications to school life: examples of it are school work accepted as a duty and done with good will; courage and perseverance when difficulties come; respect for teachers; loyalty toward and love for fellow students; sincerity, tolerance, and goodness in all relationships."

THE RELIGIOUS DIMENSION OF EDUCATION IN A CATHOLIC SCHOOL §47

1. We promote tolerance through creating a nurturing classroom environment in which we work to respect our students. We model tolerance so students will learn how to respect the differences in each other. We also set expectations regarding work ethic and behavior, and follow through consistently. How does a Catholic school community balance tolerance with setting consistent expectations for the class?

2. How can the faculty and staff promote pride in the school and pride in individual classrooms? How does teaching students to take pride in their community relate to courage, perseverance, and good will toward others?

3. Why is it important that students take ownership of their work and progress? How can teachers ensure the transition from instruction and modeling to student ownership?

4. How can the faculty and staff engage parents in a Catholic school's mission to develop students morally, socially, and academically?

JENNIFER KETCHUM

"Knowledge, values, attitudes, and behavior fully integrated with faith will result in the student's personal synthesis of life and faith. Very few Catholics, then, have the opportunity that the educator has to accomplish the very purpose of evangelization: the incarnation of the Christian message in the lives of men and women."

LAY CATHOLICS IN SCHOOLS §31

Lord,
I am ever grateful for the opportunity to spend my days forming these beautiful children in the faith, and in turn being formed through them. In answering the call to Catholic education, I have received a gift greater than any I have given.

Grant that the knowledge we share with our students be accurate and helpful, and that it inspires our students to serve You, building Your Kingdom on Earth.

Grant that our students learn values at school by watching their teachers more than by listening to our words, and that the values we teach be apparent in the way we live and work as a community.

Grant that my attitude reflect Yours in a way that will lead those in my care closer to You. If I serve You with humility and generosity, my students will do the same. May my attitude toward my vocation be a source of peace to my students as they consider the vocations to which You call them.

Grant that my behavior reflect the faith, hope, and love that I receive only through You. As we pray that You increase these virtues in each of our hearts, let my students see them embodied in me throughout our days together.

I have only a short time with my students, and I may never know of their lives as adults. Grant that the care I have

shown remain a source of hope as they mature, and guide them safely into a productive life of faith.
Amen.

MICHELLE RYAN

"As those first responsible for the education of their children, parents have the right to choose a school for them which corresponds to their own convictions. This right is fundamental. As far as possible parents have the duty of choosing schools that will best help them in their task as Christian educators. Public authorities have the duty of guaranteeing this parental right and of ensuring the concrete conditions for its exercise."

CATHECHISM OF THE CATHOLIC CHURCH §2229

For my parents, education was always a first priority. Although I lived over thirty-five miles from the nearest Catholic high school, when the public school I attended went on strike for the second year, my parents did not hesitate to transfer me. They had always wanted my siblings and me to attend a Catholic school, but the distance made it difficult. The lack of availability of Catholic education was disappointing, and as more schools close, it becomes less possible for students and parents to choose a Catholic school to attend.

My parents gave me the opportunity to attend a Catholic school despite the challenges it posed for our family, and this experience proved to be invaluable. It gave me the opportunity to grow in several ways, both mentally and spiritually, which was something that was impossible at the public school. By attending a Catholic school, I have been given a deeper understanding of my faith and an appreciation for the sacrifices that families make in choosing a Catholic school.

SORIN ENGELLAND-SPOHN

"Certainly in schools, education is essentially accomplished through teaching, which is the vehicle through which ideas and beliefs are communicated. In this sense, 'words are the main roads in educating the mind.'"

EDUCATING TOGETHER IN CATHOLIC SCHOOLS §38

1. What words should dominate our teaching in Catholic schools?

2. Note well the words you speak today. How have they educated your students? Your colleagues?

3. Christ is the Master Teacher. What words and ways of teaching did He use? How can we imitate Him?

4. Christ is the Divine Logos, the Word. All truths and words find their origin and end in Him. How can we make the unity of all truth evident to our students in all subjects? How can we relate all truth to the Truth, Jesus Christ?

SISTER JOHN PAUL MYERS, O.P.

"In catechesis it is Christ, the Incarnate Word and Son of God, who is taught—everything else is taught with reference to Him—and it is Christ alone who teaches—anyone else teaches to the extent that he is Christ's spokesman, enabling Christ to teach with his lips."

CATECHESI TRADENDAE §6

Christ, be my lips.

Send Your words through my mouth.
Send Your love through my heart.
Send Your work through my hands.
Send Your journey through my feet.

Encourage my students to walk in Your path.
Encourage my students to love one another.
Encourage my students to keep peace in the classroom.
Help us all be happy, healthy, holy, and safe.

Communicate Your Word through my lips.
You are in me, and I in You.
You are in them, too.
I see You through their smiles; Help them shine.

Christ, be my lips.

Christ, the Incarnate Word and Son of God,
Teach through me.
Amen.

CHRISTIE HJERPE

"Perfect schools are the result not so much of good methods as of good teachers, teachers who are thoroughly prepared and well-grounded in the matter they have to teach; who possess the intellectual and moral qualifications required by their important office; who cherish a pure and holy love for the youths confided to them, because they love Jesus Christ and His Church, of which these are the children of predilection; and who have therefore sincerely at heart the true good of family and country."

DIVINI ILIUS MAGISTRI §88

Special education is a field that is governed by federal and state laws. These laws are then interpreted by each school and implemented by teachers and leaders. In many cases, state and school interpretations of the laws vary and students may have special education services in one place, but then not qualify for services in another. Additionally, there is a plethora of paperwork that schools fill out with families in order to meet legal compliance. Given the many layers of complexity surrounding special education, often professionals, while well intended, are misinformed.

What I often find amazing as I work with schools, are the number of teachers who do what's best for students with exceptional needs without any training in special education, even though they do not know the legal formalities. I am additionally shocked by the number of formally trained special education teachers who adhere to the letter of the law in their paperwork, but struggle to implement best practice in their daily interactions. This passage pushes us to remember that maintaining the spirit and intent of special education legislation is more about authentic best practice, rather than arbitrary legal compliance. We as Catholics honor the dignity of the individual, and in our schools, students with exceptional needs offer us the opportunity to put these beliefs into action every day.

AZURE SMILEY

"Families, and more specifically parents, are free to choose for their children a particular kind of religious and moral education consonant with their own convictions. Even when they entrust these responsibilities to ecclesiastical institutions or to schools administered by religious personnel, their educational presence ought to continue to be constant and active."

GRATISSIMAM SANE §16

---

1. We live in a society in which children, families, and especially parents, are incredibly busy. How do you work to keep a parent's presence in the school "constant and active"?

2. As Catholic school teachers and administrators closely monitor enrollment numbers and work to keep schools open in a secular world, how can they keep Catholic identity strong while accepting an increasing number of students whose parents chose the school not for its "Catholicity" but for its strong academic qualities?

3. Is this quote still applicable given the increasing number of non-Catholic families that choose Catholic education, or does Catholic education need to change its focus and purpose to fit a changing world?

4. Sometimes parents and administrators do not always agree how best to handle a difficult situation. How do you reconcile these differences without diminishing the parents' given right and ability to be educators?

HEATHER LINDSAY

"Christian education sees all of humanity as one large family, divided perhaps by historical and political events, but always one in God who is Father of all."

THE RELIGIOUS DIMENSION OF EDUCATION IN A CATHOLIC SCHOOL §45

God Our Father,
Our nation's newcomers often face
    ridicule and discrimination.
Let Your Church
    be a place of solace and comfort
    for those that are new to our country.
Let our schools
    be places of acceptance
    for these new Americans.
Allow us
    to acknowledge the gifts and wisdom
    that these new members of our communities
    bring with them.
Guide us
    to foster relationships
    that will ensure that all
    are welcome to Your Church.
We pray in the name of Christ Jesus.
Amen.

CHRISTOPHER BOTT

"The commitment of Catholic schools to Christian values and the Christian moral code renders a profound service to society which depends on spiritual values and good moral conduct for its very survival."

TO TEACH AS JESUS DID §111

In 2007, the State of Illinois passed a law requiring a moment of silence in schools. By 2009, the law had been struck down by the courts as unconstitutional. The judge said the law was "a subtle effort to force students at impressionable ages to contemplate religion." Oh no! How awful! Regardless of one's constitutional interpretations, the judge seems to have gotten it right. A moment of silence can certainly be an opportunity for young people, at an age when so many values are formed, to "contemplate" religion. And I hope they do!

It struck me at that time how prayer is integrally interwoven into our school. Each class begins with prayer. Each lunch period begins with prayer. Sporting events begin with prayer and the opportunities for reflection, both individual and communal, are too many to count. How lucky are we to be able to pray freely and to give our students this wonderful opportunity for spiritual growth and relationship with God?

Public schools try to emulate successful religious schools by providing character education and requiring service of students. And for a few months, one state tried to require an observed moment of silence. But character education and service mandates outside of the context of community and morality are incomplete. While these goals for all students are laudable, they are not part of the fabric of the public school. We are fortunate that they are part of our mission.

DAN TULLY

21

"The educator is required to constantly update the contents of the subjects he teaches and the pedagogical methods he uses. The educator's vocation demands a ready and constant ability for renewal and adaptation."

EDUCATING TOGETHER IN CATHOLIC SCHOOLS §23

---

1. As you walk through the school today, take time to observe the teaching methodology of the teachers. Is the methodology focused on the student? Can you identify areas of growth for three teachers today?

2. Spend time at a faculty meeting discussing twenty-first century skills. Can you challenge each teacher to identify one area of growth related to these skills? How can you help this person grow in this particular area?

3. Take some time to reflect on your areas of growth. What concrete ways can you identify to assist your own growth in these areas? Make it a priority to read an article, attend a conference/workshop, or visit with a colleague to share ideas.

4. What is an area of growth for the faculty? Do not limit yourself to academics; perhaps an area of growth is in prayer or faith sharing. Make this a priority and find a way to have a speaker or take a day for communal reflection and discussion on this topic.

SISTER MARY JANE HERB, I.H.M.

"There can be no doubt whatever of the importance of the apostolate of teaching in the total saving mission of the Church."

THE CATHOLIC SCHOOL §88

Dear Lord,
Please help me today as I begin Your work shaping the minds and hearts of my students. Allow my heart to be open to You in order to learn as well as teach.

Give me the wisdom to incorporate Your words into all aspects of the curriculum today that my teaching may draw students closer to You.

Let me be like Jesus today, teaching those eager to learn, and giving them the knowledge to succeed in their every endeavor.

Let me be the hands and feet of Jesus on earth as I teach today, and enable me to spread Your word to those who need You most.

I know that with Your help, I can play a role in the mission of the Church to educate those who are most vulnerable. Give me the strength, courage, and grace today to speak Your words and bring myself and those around me closer to You.
Amen.

ANNE CHRISTINE BARBERA

"Through schools, men and women religious educate, help young people to grasp their own identity and to reveal those authentic needs and desires that inhabit everyone's heart, but which often remain unknown and underestimated: thirst for authenticity and honesty, for love and fidelity, for truth and consistency, for happiness and fullness of life. Desires which in the final analysis converge in the supreme human desire: to see the face of God."

CONSECRATED PERSONS AND THEIR MISSION IN SCHOOLS §18

J heard him coming while he was still down the hall. It was Jack. He was kicking the teacher, screaming wildly, and banging the wall whenever he could reach it. We had been through this before, but this outburst seemed worse than the others. Jack's parents, teachers, and I had tried to figure out why this blond-headed first grader, at moments so charming and docile, could fly into a rage like nothing any of us had ever seen.

He approached the office and with great effort sat in the chair, pounding his little fists on the desk and wildly kicking his feet while his eyes turned black with an inchoate rage. In the presence of this tiny child, I felt frightened. I had no idea what to do, having spent every resource in my admittedly sparse arsenal. I watched him for some time in silence and then said, "Jack, let's pray." Amazingly, he quieted down. As I asked the Lord to be with us, I watched Jack's body relax. He closed his eyes and bowed his head. His fists unclenched. When our prayer was finished, his eyes snapped open wide and he looked intently at me. Before I knew what had happened, he leaped across the table and wrapped his arms around my neck. "I want to love Jesus," he cried. "I really do! I want to be good!"

The supreme human desire: to see the face of God. We can sometimes forget that every person has this longing, to gaze upon the face that first gazed with love upon us. In rare and often unexpected moments, however, the Lord lifts the veil from His face and we can glimpse His glory.

SISTER ANNE CATHERINE BURLEIGH, O.P.

"It is essential that every possible effort be made to ensure that Catholic schools, despite financial difficulties, continue to provide 'a Catholic education to the poor and the marginalized in society.' It will never be possible to free the needy from their poverty unless they are first freed from the impoverishment arising from the lack of adequate education."

ECCLESIA IN AMERICA §71

---

1. What connections are there between education and freedom?

2. In what ways have you been empowered and freed through your commitment to Catholic schools?

3. How do you envision your vocation as a Catholic school educator to be a part of your response to the Catholic Church's social teaching?

4. How is Catholic education distinct from other forms of education in relation to the poor and marginalized in society?

5. What is the relationship between material poverty (e.g., lack of nutrition, clothing, and shelter) and spiritual poverty manifest in ignorance, apathy, consumerism, and individualism? How does Catholic education free one from these poverties?

MAX ENGEL

"[Catholic schools] are significantly effective in preparing students for life in today's Church and society. They instill in children and young people indispensable discipline of mind and heart. They have a highly positive impact on adult religious behavior."

TEACH THEM! §11

Lord,
We thank You for calling our students closer to You and toward a Catholic education, where they have opportunities to develop their academic and religious understanding.

You encourage them during their academic endeavors, and we thank You for being with them thus far in the wonder and challenge of their schooling.

They are blessed to be surrounded by people who are vehicles of grace in this stage of their lifelong development to be active members of the Church.

Learning about and participating in the sacraments, service, and worship bring them closer to You each day. Let them use their education to strengthen their talents and do Your will now and after graduation.

Strengthen them to live out the promise that they made to You and to themselves when they enrolled in a Catholic school—to embrace the opportunities in this academic environment and to challenge the depths of their faith. Thank You for being by their side as they ask questions and learn, as they doubt and develop their religious behavior.

Help them to graduate this place with more than a diploma, with a stronger and more confident understanding of the Church and devotion to You.

Thank You for helping them to see that as they study with their minds, they may also learn with their heart.

In Your name, we pray.
Amen.

MELISSA REGAN

"For parents by themselves are not capable of satisfying every requirement of the whole process of raising children, especially in matters concerning their schooling and the entire gamut of socialization. Subsidiarity thus complements paternal and maternal love and confirms its fundamental nature, inasmuch as all other participants in the process of education are only able to carry out their responsibilities in the name of the parents, with their consent and, to a certain degree, with their authorization."

GRATISSIMAM SANE §16

$\mathcal{I}$ never considered the tremendous challenge it must have been for my parents to entrust my education to others. They blithely sent me off to kindergarten on a yellow bus carrying the obligatory red lunchbox, the moment preserved in a single photograph of a smiling five-year-old at the end of a gravel driveway, waving to the people behind the camera. And they've done the same thing every year since; taken a picture and waved me away to years of elementary school, junior high, high school, and now college. In this time, I've come to realize that this is both an act of love and faith. They love me enough to recognize the value in a great education, and they have chosen to have faith in the educational institutions that I attend. They participate in my education by allowing me to explore and learn in places outside of the home. It is this partnership between my parents and my educators that has given me the best possibility for knowledge, and I am eternally grateful to both.

RACHEL ROSEBERRY

"This integration of religious truth and values with the rest of life is brought about in the Catholic school not only by its unique curriculum but, more important, by the presence of teachers who express an integrated approach to learning and living in their private and professional lives."

TO TEACH AS JESUS DID §104

---

1. Do I teach the students in my care to think critically when faced with choices that compromise who they are?

2. As teachers and administrators, God calls us to Catholic schools with the purpose of sharing our faith in every interaction with our students. How do I interject the call to social justice in math class, in language arts, indeed in every subject area, not just religion?

3. We live in an increasingly global community. How do I encourage my students to serve not only the child in the next desk, but also the suffering members of the community and the world? Do I provide them with opportunities to serve others and do I model service to others on a global stage?

KATHY ASMAR

"Intimately linked in charity to one another and to their students and endowed with an apostolic spirit, may teachers by their life as much as by their instruction bear witness to Christ, the unique Teacher."

GRAVISSIMUM EDUCATIONIS §8

Father God,
One of my greatest daily struggles comes in the challenge of modeling Your compassion for all who need Your loving embrace.

As an educator often burdened with the happenings that clutter every school day, it is easy to lose my focus and overlook the opportunities which are present to demonstrate Your love in any of a variety of forms to those children placed in my care.

Give me the strength and the vigilance to be attentive to the times when I might best manifest Your loving kindness by word or deed and thereby bear witness to Your presence in the lives of those whom I serve.

Help me to see those who are in need of Your healing touch and to refrain from harsh words or actions which are so damaging to relationships.

I genuinely want to be Your voice and Your touch to these children and ask Your guidance that I may emulate Your example as teacher, friend, and parent.

Bless those whom I serve with open ears, eyes, and hearts that they may also be inspired to live with that same readiness for compassion.
Amen.

SARAH WATSON

"[The Catholic school] must develop persons who are responsible and inner-directed, capable of choosing freely in conformity with their conscience. This is simply another way of saying that the school is an institution where young people gradually learn to open themselves up to life as it is, and to create in themselves a definite attitude to life as it should be."

THE CATHOLIC SCHOOL §31

The streets off of Interstate 94 in North Minneapolis run alphabetically east to west. Aldridge, Bryant, Colfax and so on down the line. When I was living there as a volunteer, the streets also became more dangerous and the buildings more dilapidated the farther down the alphabet you traveled. It was in this neighborhood, on North Queen Avenue, that I coordinated a summer program for Catholic youth to live in the city and volunteer at a variety of social service organizations.

Most of the young men and women who volunteered were from the suburbs, nearly all attended suburban Catholic schools, and many never knew of the poverty that was just a short drive from their homes and schools. There was certainly some shock as the teens came to grips with a life so foreign, yet so proximate, to their own.

What struck me as the weeks progressed was that these young women and men were not stymied by the injustices they witnessed, but were resolved to meet them head on. Serving meals at the downtown shelter, taking children who were homeless to swim at the "fancy" YMCA, running a summer program for children from low-income families, listening, welcoming, feeding, visiting, and the list goes on. Over the course of a summer it was clear to me that these young adults had a vision of "life as it should be" that was informed and animated by the Gospel, at the core of their Catholic school experiences, and a manifestation of the Gospel command to care for "the least of these brothers of mine" (Mt 25:40).

ANTHONY HOLTER

"In virtue of its mission, then, the school must be concerned with constant and careful attention to cultivating in students the intellectual, creative, and aesthetic faculties of the human person; to develop in them the ability to make correct use of their judgment, will, and affectivity; to promote in them a sense of values; to encourage just attitudes and prudent behavior; to introduce them to the cultural patrimony handed down from previous generations; to prepare them for professional life, and to encourage the friendly interchange among students of diverse cultures and backgrounds that will lead to mutual understanding. For all of these reasons, the school enters into the specific mission of the Church."

LAY CATHOLICS IN SCHOOLS §12

---

1. Is cultural diversity reflected throughout the entire curriculum?

2. Many Catholic school and parish communities have unique traditions. How are these incorporated into the classroom, and why would this be of value?

3. Does the educational program foster lifelong learning and personal growth? How does the faculty help the students develop a sense of the intrinsic value of learning?

4. Beyond respect and understanding of other cultures, how can the school community build a learning environment that prepares students to develop into world citizens who recognize their role in creating a fairer, more equitable society?

JENNIFER KETCHUM

"The tendency to adopt present-day values as a yardstick is not absent even in the educational world. The danger is always to react to passing, superficial ideas and to lose sight of the much deeper needs of the contemporary world."

THE CATHOLIC SCHOOL §30

Giving Lord,
Our Catholic schools mean so much to us,
    Providing the avenue to Your word;
    Educating in the ways of Your world;
    Nurturing Your children;
    Embracing those who need us most;
    Loving all that life has to offer.
Allow our leaders to make wise choices;
    Lead our parents to make good decisions;
    And enable us to be good stewards of Your gifts.
We ask this through Jesus Christ our Lord.
Amen.

CHRISTOPHER BOTT

"From the first moment that a student sets foot in a Catholic school, he or she ought to have the impression of entering a new environment, one illuminated by the light of faith, and having its own unique characteristics."

THE RELIGIOUS DIMENSION OF EDUCATION IN A CATHOLIC SCHOOL §25

The true magic of a Catholic school is not noticeable upon first glance. The building stands like any other school, filled with students to be taught, books to be read, and schedules to be met.

However, upon closer examination, there are many subtle signs that lead to a marked difference in environment. In the case of my high school these differences were the small crucifixes in every room, the daily prayer broadcast over the intercom, and the ministry office tucked behind the second stairwell. These tangible things, however small, were manifestations of other, more important, differences: the feeling of collective support, the sense of responsibility to others, and the knowledge that our learning was for something more than just college admission. These differences were the ones that greeted visitors at the door, calling and welcoming them into the community.

We must keep these small differences in mind and realize that they are the reason for this school and its unique character. So often, it is easy to let daily concerns impede our view of what is important. We must be careful not to let the world taint this special faith environment but instead try to bring our small differences into the world.

The Catholic school, then, has two purposes: to create a unique and faith-filled environment for the cultivation of its students and to inspire these students to take what they learn and share it with the world. We must wake up with the realization of both these goals and the resolve to see them through.

LAURA CASSEL

"The Church is bound as a mother to give to these children of hers an education by which their whole life can be imbued with the spirit of Christ and at the same time do all she can to promote for all peoples the complete perfection of the human person, the good of earthly society and the building of a world that is more human."

GRAVISSIMUM EDUCATIONIS §3

---

1. What responsibilities does the parish community have to support Catholic education? What is your experience of this kind of support in your parish?

2. How do you invite the larger church community to partner with the school community to provide educational and/or spiritual opportunities for the students, faculty, and staff?

3. What do you do at your school to model the spirit of Christ for students, parents, the larger church community, and each other on the faculty or staff?

4. How would you define a world that is "more human"? What is your school community doing to help build a world like that?

SISTER BARBARA KANE, O.P.

"Those who are dedicated to the work of education, particularly of the young, or who mold public opinion should consider it their most weighty task to instruct all in fresh sentiments of peace."

GAUDIUM ET SPES §82

Lord Jesus,
In word and deed, You led a life of service committed to justice and peace. In Your earthly ministry, You were friend to sinner and saint, and have instructed us to pray even for those who persecute us.

You challenge us to reflect a love so great that it includes our enemies. Even as You faced unjust persecution, You modeled Your commitment to non-violent love through Your passion and death. Inspired by the triumph of peace over death in the Resurrection, may our Catholic schools produce future leaders committed to resolving situations of conflict through peaceful means.

We pray first for the adoption of peace in our lives—in our homes and in our schools. May we treat our families, our fellow staff members, and our students with the love and peace that You modeled for us. May we also boldly carry this message of peace to our war-weary and environmentally-torn world. May our schools infuse the Gospel message of peace to the far reaches of the earth.

May our faith in You inspire and sustain our efforts to build peace in our hearts and in our world.
Amen.

PETER CORRIGAN

"When it is animated by lay and consecrated persons that live the same educational mission in sincere unity, the Catholic school shows the face of a community that tends towards an increasingly deeper communion."

EDUCATING TOGETHER IN CATHOLIC SCHOOLS §55

---

*I*deally, a Catholic school setting should be a place where the students can see lived out the various states of life in the Church. A parish school, in particular, can be a place to experience the lively interplay of priests, religious, and laity all working and worshipping together. Several years ago during Catholic Schools Week, our elementary school decided to host an all-school faith rally. Centered upon Eucharistic Adoration and the sacraments, we wanted to create an opportunity where the students, their parents, and parishioners young and old could really encounter the living Jesus within the context of true *communio*.

One particular memory from the day remains etched in my mind. After organizing the students into multi-age "families" for catechesis sessions and activities, the entire school convened in the gym for Eucharistic Adoration. It was no small feat to have over 200 students from Grades 1 to 8 kneeling quietly on mats on the floor for close to an hour. Yet that is exactly what they were doing, accompanied by many parents, teachers, and sisters, as well as a group of elderly parishioners beaming from chairs behind the students. A group of local high school students, most of whom were graduates of the school, led the students in praise and worship, while the pastor took the Blessed Sacrament from atop the massive "burning bush" flickering with votive lights and began to process through the crowd. Children spontaneously bowed low to the ground as the Lord passed by. The faces of sometimes stoic teachers assumed an awed expression marked by tears, while parents who had not frequented the Sacrament of Reconciliation in years made their way to the priests who had joined us from the neighboring parishes.

What a witness of true communion! For a few graced moments, parents forgot their complaints and teachers realized capacities they had never witnessed in their students. The young people were opened up to the beauty of friendship with God while the older people were invited to renew a relationship that had perhaps grown routine. Thanks to the conduit of the Catholic school, everyone—the priests, the religious sisters, students, and the families—experienced in a very concrete way what it means to be the Body of Christ.

SISTER ANNE CATHERINE BURLEIGH, O.P.

"It is, then, incumbent on parents to strain every nerve to ward off such an outrage, and to strive manfully to have and to hold exclusive authority to direct the education of their offspring, as is fitting, in a Christian manner, and first and foremost to keep them away from schools where there is risk of their drinking in the poison of impiety."

SAPIENTIAE CHRISTIANAE §42

1. With Catholic schools closing and becoming less accessible in certain parts of the country, how can parents ensure exclusive authority over the education of their children?

2. How can parents maintain this influence once the child is in school in order to eliminate risks of poor influences even within a Christian environment?

3. How do Catholic educators reduce impious influences within a school setting in order to provide a healthy environment for students?

SARAH WATSON

"Teachers' life style and character are as important as their professional credentials."

TEACH THEM! §29

Heavenly Father,
It's a truism that we teach who we are.

It's also humbling when former students tell me how important my classes were to them, but can't recall much of the academic material.

I know all my training, planning, and preparation were not in vain—that effort made possible the atmosphere of thinking and questioning that resulted in students learning about themselves and the world as they gained knowledge and skills.

I pray for:
    Good friends and colleagues
        who help me be the person I was created to be;
    Wisdom in helping my students
        grow as people and learners;
    Awareness that everything I do,
        whether in class or by myself, testifies to You;
    Guidance to therefore always do the truth
        so I may witness to the truth that is Yours.
Amen.

MAX ENGEL

"Like the mission and message of Jesus Christ, the Church's educational mission is universal—for all men, at all times, in all places. In our world and in our nation, the mission of Christian education is of critical importance. The truth of Jesus Christ must be taught; the love of Jesus Christ must be extended to persons who seek and suffer."

TO TEACH AS JESUS DID §154

As I sit at the conference room table listening to the great ideas from the facilitator, my mind wanders to a different place. The topic is the future of Catholic education in our diocese, but the discussion has branched off into a political debate regarding finances. I think of my son, a Pre-K student at a local Catholic school, imagining what his school will look like in ten years. What types of experiences will he be exposed to? How will Scripture, service to others, liturgy, and academics be presented to him?

The questions linger on and the conversation at the table gets back on track. We discuss the long and storied histories of several of the schools that have closed in recent years. I get goose bumps envisioning Catholic schools with 150-year histories closing their doors forever. I drift again thinking of the incredible positions that our Church leaders, school leaders, parents, and students are put into regarding our Catholic schools.

Our needs are great during this pivotal time in the history of American Catholic education. While we have no secret formula or silver bullet, we do have each other. Our mission to teach the truth and love of Jesus Christ must continue, regardless of circumstances or problems. Let us use the gifts that have been bestowed upon us to develop and implement strategies to ensure that Catholic education endures for generations to come.

CHRISTOPHER BOTT

"The family has the responsibility to provide an integral education. Indeed, all true education 'is directed towards the formation of the human person in view of his final end and the good of that society to which he belongs and in the duties of which he will, as an adult, have a share.' This integrality is ensured when children—with the witness of life and in words—are educated in dialogue, encounter, sociality, legality, solidarity and peace, through the cultivation of the fundamental virtues of justice and charity."

COMPENDIUM OF THE SOCIAL DOCTRINE OF THE CHURCH §242

Dear Lord,
The Church reminds us that parents are the primary educators of their children.

The school's responsibility is to support and extend the education that begins at home. The formation of our students as Christians relies in part on the education we provide.

What do my students witness in my life and hear in my words? I see You in each of them; each of us was made in Your image, and I love You in them. Do they see my love for You in my actions? Do they hear Your words from my mouth?

Lord, lead me in a life that cultivates my own virtues. You call me daily to prayer, to good works, to the sacraments, but I don't always answer the call. Please open my ears and my heart to Your invitation, so that through a rich prayer life and a dedication to Your work, I can receive the graces I most need.

I pray daily that you grant me faith, hope, and love, and I pray now that these virtues in me help form the students in my care.

Finally, Lord, keep the passion for education alive in me
so that, through my own learning, I can lead the teachers
and students of my school in a well-rounded education by
which they can serve You.
Amen.

MICHELLE RYAN

*"Every school and every place of non formal education can
become a centre of a greater network which, from the small-
est village to the most complex metropolis, wraps the world
in hope. It is in education, in fact, that the promise of a more
human future and a more harmonious society lies."*

CONSECRATED PERSONS AND THEIR MISSION IN SCHOOLS §84

1. How does the Gospel serve to civilize humanity?

2. What does a "more human future" look like? How can
   our schools and classrooms become more human?

3. How is Christian hope different from the hope the
   world offers our students and communities?

4. Why is peace a natural fruit of a Catholic school
   education? Is peace tangible in your school? What can
   you do to cultivate a culture of love?

SISTER JOHN PAUL MYERS, O.P.

"It teaches one how to be a member of the wider social communities; and when the educational community is at the same time a Christian community—and this is what the educational community of a Catholic school must always be striving toward—then it offers a great opportunity for the teachers to provide the students with a living example of what it means to be a member of that great community which is the Church."

LAY CATHOLICS IN SCHOOLS §21

While debate in the U.S. continues, and pundits and politicians discuss the moral and legal dilemma of our current immigration issue, the children of the immigrants in question are very likely sitting in the classrooms of our Catholic schools.

In my local community, the INS staged one of the largest raids of its time on a business, looking for illegal immigrants working in its factories. Many of the children of the suspected immigrants were students in my school. I lost children whose families moved to other areas to avoid detection. I had children whose parents were arrested and sent to federal facilities, or who were put under house arrest and required to wear a monitoring device until their case came to trial.

The children were confused and scared. School, for them, offered a safe haven for eight hours a day. While their future in the United States is uncertain, we must remember that for the present we are in the unique position of making a difference in children's lives.

While debate swirls around us, inside the school, we are charged with bringing children into the faith-filled Catholic community where there is total acceptance and love for one another's uniqueness and giftedness. The situation also presents us with the opportunity to teach love and acceptance of all God's children to the children of families who are not directly touched by the current immigration issues.

KATHY ASMAR

"It is the responsibility of the entire Catholic community—bishops, priests, deacons, religious, and laity—to continue to strive towards the goal of making our Catholic elementary and secondary schools available, accessible, and affordable to all Catholic parents and their children, including those who are poor and middle class."

RENEWING OUR COMMITMENT p. 1

God of Justice and Compassion,
You revealed Yourself long ago as the God of the oppressed and poor, liberating Your people from suffering and bondage. Hear our prayers in this modern age where children still go hungry, where injustices still abound, and countless people never learn of Your love.

In our efforts to make justice flow like a river, we have sacrificed much to build Catholic schools. We know them to be places of community and faith, learning and light. Open our eyes to see the needs of all who suffer, our ears to hear the cries of the poor, our hearts to feel the anguish of those who do not know You.

On us the poor have special claims; with them we strive to lift all Your people out of poverty and into the light of Your Kingdom. Through Catholic education and in Catholic schools, let Your children be embraced and welcomed. Give courage and wisdom to all people of good will, so that they may see these schools as instruments of grace and temples of Your glory, for in access to Catholic schools, O Lord, we find access to You.
Amen.

FATHER RONALD NUZZI

"The right and duty of parents to give education is essential, since it is connected with the transmission of human life; it is original and primary with regard to the educational role of others, on account of the uniqueness of the loving relationship between parents and children; and it is irreplaceable and inalienable, and therefore incapable of being entirely delegated to others or usurped by others."

FAMILIARIS CONSORTIO §36

---

1. The original and primary role of educator belongs to parents, but parents also entrust the expansion of their child's education to Catholic school teachers. Do you recognize this by striving to include parents in their child's education in school and maintaining a relationship with those parents? Do you encourage parents to stay involved in their child's education and create opportunities for parents to do so?

2. Education of a child requires not just the development of one's knowledge in areas like mathematics, science, and history, but also the development of the whole person. Do you link your teaching to the development of the student? How can you improve your efforts to foster well-rounded students?

3. Since a child's family does hold the primary obligation to educate, it is important to maintain that familial environment in school. In order for students to be engaged in their learning, they must feel like they are welcomed and belong. Do you make an effort to create a positive environment for your students while maintaining the importance of their education? Are there some students who need more guidance in adjusting to this environment? How can you better integrate them into the classroom and with their peers?

KEVIN KIMBERLY

"Parents are the first and most important educators of their own children, and they also possess a fundamental competence in this area: they are educators because they are parents. They share their educational mission with other individuals or institutions, such as the Church and the State. But the mission of education must always be carried out in accordance with a proper application of the principle of subsidiarity. This implies the legitimacy and indeed the need of giving assistance to the parents, but finds its intrinsic and absolute limit in their prevailing right and their actual capabilities."

GRATISSIMAM SANE §16

J was recently at a meeting with principals from around California and someone made the comment, "sometimes I just wish I worked in an orphanage." This was in reference to the difficulty teachers and principals sometimes encounter when working with the parents of the students they serve. While not meant to be taken literally, it does drive home the point that for many educators, working with parents can be the biggest challenge they face in a sea of challenges. I have heard people blame it on feelings of entitlement or the disconnect between parents and what teachers and principals really face each day. While these are valid hypotheses, the bottom line is that we are not mechanics servicing cars or bankers dealing with money. We are educators serving the most loved and cherished gift that God can bestow in a parent's life, a child.

As Catholic school educators, the need to collaborate and work with parents is more than just a good educational practice. It is a calling to understand that by the very nature of having a child, the parents we serve are educators who are experts in their own children. We are called by God to support parents in the education of their children by celebrating successes, gently guiding when we perceive a problem, and most importantly listening intently when they have a concern. After many difficult conversations with parents, I understand how challenging this can be, but any relationship is made easier when we invite God to be part of the process.

PAMELA LYONS

"For every educator is in need of humility in order to recognize one's own limitations, one's mistakes, along with the need for constant growth, and the realization that the ideal being pursued is always beyond one's grasp."

LAY CATHOLICS IN SCHOOLS §72

Heavenly Father,
Help me to understand my limitations and the expanses where I am incomplete.

Give me the humility to acknowledge that just as I ask my students to be lifelong learners, so must I work to continuously grow.

Understanding that I must continue to nurture my intellect as well as my spirituality gives me reason to read, cooperate, learn, and pray to improve myself. Knowing that I am never perfect gives me the humility to ask for help.

There are days, weeks or even months, when I am tired and drained. Allow me to be energized to continue my personal and professional growth.

Help me to know that I am never alone in my work, but that You are at my side.

As I realize my work is for You, I am granted the patience and openness to always seek self-improvement, for as much as I am a teacher, I am also a student.
Amen.

DAN TULLY

"Therefore, the formational experience of the Catholic school constitutes an impressive barrier against the influence of a widespread mentality that leads young people especially 'to consider themselves and their lives as a series of sensations to be experienced rather than as a work to be accomplished.'"

EDUCATING TOGETHER IN CATHOLIC SCHOOLS §42

---

1. What is the mentality of contemporary culture that leads young people to view life as "a series of sensations" to be experienced?

2. What formational experiences should a Catholic school provide to enable students to see their lives as a vocation, a calling, that is, a journey to God to be travelled in the context of the community of faith?

3. What should a Catholic school do to create an understanding of and foster a consideration by students of not only the vocation of marriage or the single life but also of priesthood and the consecrated life?

BROTHER WILLIAM DYGERT, C.S.C.

"With its educational project inspired by the Gospel, the Catholic school is called to take up this challenge and respond to it in the conviction that it is only in the mystery of the Word made flesh that the mystery of man truly becomes clear."

THE CATHOLIC SCHOOL ON THE THRESHOLD OF THE THIRD MILLENNIUM §10

Lord,
Sometimes it is not clear what You want of me.
I cannot see the road ahead and I am unsure of my actions.
Help me to embrace the questions and to trust in You,
Because You always know what is best for me.

Illuminate my duty through the Gospel
And the example of Christ on earth.
May I rise to the challenges You set before me
Confident that You will not give me anything
I am not capable of handling.

Bless all my actions with the conviction You exemplified
That I may find my calling in following You
And encourage others to do the same.
Amen.

LAURA CASSEL

"These Catholic schools afford the fullest and best opportunity to realize the fourfold purpose of Christian education, namely to provide an atmosphere in which the Gospel message is proclaimed, community in Christ is experienced, service to our sisters and brothers is the norm, and thanksgiving and worship of our God is cultivated."

RENEWING OUR COMMITMENT p. 1

How do students encounter these four initiatives at school? What is their role, as students, to embrace these purposes for their own growth and also to foster their prevalence among their peers?

First, an atmosphere where the Gospel message is proclaimed is something deserving profound appreciation—a step back on students' part, to listen and reflect in a community that encourages just this kind of receiving of the Word.

Students must also embrace the community that surrounds them, the common mission to experience Christ, so that it can strengthen them and they can contribute to the community experience of their peers.

Third, service is often the norm at some schools, but what are individual students doing in response? Are they centered in selfless service? Do they feed off this energy to accomplish service and also to sustain the atmosphere of giving?

And last, students should spend time thanking and worshiping God, for all that He has given and will continue to give. Students must ask how they, now, can respond best to their gifts—which are only possible in Him—and then carry all that they develop into the world after graduation.

MELISSA REGAN

"Thus, while policies and opportunities differ from place to place, the Catholic school has its place in any national school system ... in this way she helps to promote that freedom of teaching which champions and guarantees freedom of conscience and the parental right to choose the school best suited to parents' educational purpose."

THE CATHOLIC SCHOOL §14

Heavenly Father,
Thank You for the opportunity to work in a Catholic school.
By granting my coworkers and me the chance to shape
young minds, You have shaped our lives.

Continue to bless our school so that we may bring more
families closer to You. Please grant that the future will hold
prosperity for our school that we may continue to provide
students and families with the choice to attend our school.

Give our faculty the strength and courage to speak
out against policies that would harm our school and
compromise our mission.

Continue to bless all Catholic schools with the ability to
provide a faith-filled and holistic education for all children.
Amen.

SORIN ENGELLAND-SPOHN

"It is therefore as important to make no mistake in education, as it is to make no mistake in the pursuit of the last end, with which the whole work of education is intimately and necessarily connected. In fact, since education consists essentially in preparing man for what he must be and for what he must do here below, in order to attain the sublime end for which he was created, it is clear that there can be no true education which is not wholly directed to man's last end."

DIVINI ILIUS MAGISTRI §7

Catholic education was always foreign to me. I grew up in a Methodist church and attended public school through senior year of high school. My concept of schooling was bound up in the daily rituals of bells and lockers, seventh period algebra, and conversations in the lunchroom. Education was never anything more than something to be attained in the moment. The pursuit of good grades and honors classifications seemed enough of a goal in and of themselves.

Then I came to Notre Dame; a college I chose more for its Midwestern familiarity than for any other reason. I stumbled upon Catholic education and in return I was given an education premised on the fact that education is more than just immediately consequential. Education is instead eternally consequential, that is, it should prepare us to live a life that leads to the eternal. The Catholicity of this university has deepened my belief in the necessity of education. The work we do in our classes, in our conversations, in our attainment of knowledge is almost terrifyingly important because as we shape the way we think, we shape the way we pursue our "last end." This larger purpose is never easily evident sitting in the library at 1:00 a.m., frantically filling pages with words to finish a ten-page paper or cramming for the 8:00 a.m. Organic Chemistry midterm, but it's an omnipresent characteristic of this education.

The Catholic nature of education has given us the possibility for an education that matters more, and it is up to each one of us to take advantage of that.

RACHEL ROSEBERRY

"The Catholic school participates in the evangelizing mission of the Church and is the privileged environment in which Christian education is carried out."

THE CATHOLIC SCHOOL ON THE THRESHOLD OF THE THIRD MILLENNIUM §11

Heavenly Father,
Let our school be a nurturing environment in which
students can grow closer to You.

Help us to give them the ability to find You in all things,
and to see You in all people.

Please grant us the opportunity to work together as a
school to fulfill Your mission for the Church by welcoming
the unfamiliar and serving those in need.

Grant that our teachers may speak Your words and our
students may open their hearts to hear You more clearly.

Please make our school community a calming place for
those seeking peace, and an enriching place for those
seeking Your presence in all things.

Allow students to foster in each other a deeper
appreciation for all of Your children by finding Jesus in each
and every person.
Amen.

ANNE CHRISTINE BARBERA

"Education can play an outstanding role in promoting the inculturation of the Gospel."

ECCLESIA IN AMERICA §71

---

1. Take time at the end of the day today and reflect on your day. How did you give witness to the Good News of the Gospel message?

2. As you are walking through the classrooms, see the teachers through the lens of the Gospel. What Gospel passage comes to mind when you see the teacher interact with the students, in and outside of the classroom? Take time to share this insight with the teacher with a short note or an email.

3. As you plan the next faculty meeting, take time to read the daily readings or the readings for the upcoming Sunday. Incorporate these readings in the prayer at the beginning or end of the faculty meeting. If you invite the teachers to share in the preparation of prayer, encourage them to do the same.

SISTER MARY JANE HERB, I.H.M.

"Lay Catholic teachers should be influenced by a Christian faith vision in the way they teach their course, to the extent that this is consistent with the subject matter, and the circumstances of the student body and the school. In doing this, they will help students to discover true human values; and even though they must work within the limitations proper to a school that makes no attempt to educate in the faith, in which many factors will actually work directly against faith education, they will still be able to contribute to the beginnings of a dialogue between faith and culture."

LAY CATHOLICS IN SCHOOLS §49

As a special educator, I often work with families that were dealt difficult situations to navigate. These family situations are often compounded by a lack of resources in both the home and school to handle the intense issues they are facing. In all cases, both the school staff and the families are good people with good intentions. Unfortunately, my students often struggle with decision making, organization, and impulse control; all behaviors that eventually lead to emotionally charged interactions. In many cases, after poor choices made by the student, the families and school staff struggle to work together in a productive way to reconcile differences. In many cases, people begin pointing fingers and blaming each other.

After one extremely tense and nasty meeting between a family and teacher I both liked and respected, I felt exceptionally defeated. I spoke with my priest who reminded me that the blame game wasn't new; it in fact originated in the Garden of Eden. As he pointed out, it didn't work then and it doesn't work today. The simple reminder of a Bible story I had heard since I was a child was powerful to me. I internalized the idea that as long as I am blaming others, I will never be able to reflect on my own practice or solutions to the problem being faced.

We in education have a habit of falling into the blame game. Whether it is blaming parents, blaming teachers, blaming principals, blaming policymakers, or blaming funding, we often spend too much time discussing why it is someone else's fault that we can't do our jobs. I am tired of blaming everyone. I am ready to own my part and focus on what I can do to make the lives of students, families, and my community better.

I believe as Catholic educators we are called to serve and work diligently toward solutions, not judging others. Whether or not I agree with the choices of my colleagues, students, or their families should not be the focus of my behavior or choices. I choose to change the culture and climate of my school by pushing myself to reflect Catholic values, not judging others, and being self-reflective every day.

AZURE SMILEY

"The fact that in their own individual ways all members of the school community share this Christian vision makes the school 'Catholic'; principles of the Gospel in this manner become the educational norms since the school then has them as its internal motivation and final goal."

THE CATHOLIC SCHOOL §34

---

1. How can we promote a Christian community in our schools? In what ways can we strengthen the Christian community that is already in place?

2. How can the Christian community of our schools interact with the wider community of secular education and secular society?

RACHEL ROSEBERRY

"The Catholic school community, therefore, is an irreplaceable source of service, not only to the pupils and its other members, but also to society. Today especially one sees a world which clamors for solidarity and yet experiences the rise of new forms of individualism. Society can take note from the Catholic school that it is possible to create true communities out of a common effort for the common good."

THE CATHOLIC SCHOOL §62

Lord,
We know we are naturally inclined to solidarity, unity, and friendship. Our society clamors for communities, neighborhoods, and personal connections. Yet, our society also values individualism, self-sufficiency, and independence.

So we forget our inclination to solidarity, unity, and friendship. We seem confused, a bit like St. Paul who did not do the good he wanted but the evil he did not want.

Lord, remind us in Catholic school communities that our best inclinations to community and friendship are gifts from You to lead us to You. St. Paul, inspired by the spirit of life in Jesus Christ, moved beyond his individualism and self-sufficiency to bring others to life in Christ.

Help us recognize that the need for community, neighborhoods, and friendship is the drive for love and the common good that You instill in each of us.

It is in this love that we make Jesus present in the world and witness most clearly to the possibility of life lived for the common good in the Kingdom of God.
Amen.

MAX ENGEL

"In its ecclesial dimension another characteristic of the Catholic school has its root: it is a school for all, with special attention to those who are weakest."

THE CATHOLIC SCHOOL ON THE THRESHOLD OF THE THIRD MILLENIUM §15

As director of admissions, part of my job is to help determine the makeup of each class that is enrolled at our school. The hardest moments in this process occur when I have to speak to a family whose child has spent ten years in a Catholic grade school and is not admitted to a Catholic high school. Most of the time it is because the child has needs that our school cannot adequately serve.

This situation happens all over the country. There are Catholic high schools that have wonderful programs for students with special needs; however, they are too few. The reason for the dearth of programs is usually money.

Financial challenges are nothing new to Catholic schools. But we have met many of those challenges head on. Financial aid programs are almost ubiquitous; many schools are paying just wages to their teachers. Perhaps our next challenge is to answer the call of this document and make our schools places where we really do pay special attention to those who are weakest in whatever form.

PATRICK FENNESSY

"Community is at the heart of Christian education not simply as a concept to be taught but as a reality to be lived."

TO TEACH AS JESUS DID §23

Often the role of community building gets shifted solely to the principal. In reality, though, it is the job of every person involved in a school to help build community.

1. Discuss with a colleague ways they have seen you help build community in your school. Listen to their answers and use them to help guide you to make your efforts more transparent or see how you are building community in ways in which you may have been unaware.

This quote comes from the section of the document focused on the importance of building community. The section begins with a quote from the Gospel according to John: "I give you a new commandment: Love one another. Such as my love has been for you, so must your love be for each other. This is how all will know you for my disciples: your love for another" (13: 34-35).

2. Do you see the demonstration of love for others as a motivator for, pillar of, or product of the building of community in school?

The document continues to say, "Through education, men must be moved to build community in all areas of life; they do this best if they have learned the meaning of community by experiencing it. Formed by this experience, they are better able to build community in their families, their places of work, their neighborhoods, their nation, their world."

3. Looking at your school, does the community experienced there demonstrate for your students what community truly should look like?

4. Will students and staff be able to take specific encounters they have seen or experienced at school and apply them to experiences in the broader community? What makes you think so?

5. What could you do to better help your school demonstrate a vibrant Christian community to your students?

HEATHER LINDSAY

"Since its educational goals are rooted in Christian principles, the school as a whole is inserted into the evangelical function of the Church."

THE RELIGIOUS DIMENSION OF EDUCATION IN A CATHOLIC SCHOOL §69

In the footsteps of Peter,
In the spirit of Paul,
In the words of Matthew, Mark, Luke, and John,
In the way of Jesus the Christ,
May we too serve as evangelists,
Heralding the Kingdom of God.
Amen.

JIM FRABUTT

"One must recognize that, more than ever before, a Catholic school's job is infinitely more difficult, more complex, since this is a time when Christianity demands to be clothed in fresh garments, when all manner of changes have been introduced in the Church and in secular life, and, particularly, when a pluralist mentality dominates and the Christian Gospel is increasingly pushed to the side-lines."

THE CATHOLIC SCHOOL §66

J take a break from my mundane paperwork to enjoy the aroma of freshly cut grass through my office window. I observe a group of twenty students enjoying the beautiful weather during their lunch period. A teacher stands with them, laughing as he converses with them. As I observe, I have an internal conversation with myself about the intangible rewards of being a Catholic school leader.

My moment of serenity is interrupted when our school's administrative assistant knocks on the door and informs me that my 12:30 appointment has arrived. I snap back into reality, make myself presentable, clean up my desk, and depart my office to meet this prospective student and her father.

Once seated in my office, the father begins by stating, "We want to be honest and upfront with you. Our family is seeking the best educational option available to our daughter, but we are not religious people. We would prefer if she was not exposed to your theology curriculum or prayer services."

The response is automatic, having surfaced on numerous occasions in recent years. I state, "Catholicism is not an event or a course at our school. It permeates all that we do and all that we believe as a Catholic institution. We make links to God and the Catholic Church in every area of every discipline at our school. We have several non-Catholics at our school that embrace this concept and thrive as students. I do not think that our school is the right fit for your family if this concept makes you at all uncomfortable."

A bit surprised, the father continues politely with his questions. In the end, the family chose to continue in their public school.

CHRISTOPHER BOTT

"No less than other schools does the Catholic school pursue cultural goals and the human formation of youth. But its proper function is to create for the school community a special atmosphere animated by the Gospel spirit of freedom and charity, to help youth grow according to the new creatures they were made through baptism as they develop their own personalities, and finally to order the whole of human culture to the news of salvation so that the knowledge the students gradually acquire of the world, life and man is illumined by faith."

GRAVISSIMUM EDUCATIONIS §8

Heavenly Father,
Be with me each day as I lead my faculty.

Remind me that to build a vocation takes time, patience, and consistent effort.

Help me to be the leader who encourages, supports, but gently demands excellence in all that we do.

Give me the energy and enthusiasm I need to encourage professional growth from my staff.

As I meet with parents, let my words and actions facilitate the partnership that the faculty deserves.

Help me always to listen with open ears, observe with clear eyes, and speak with compassion and humility.

Let me always remember that while my words may be forgotten, my actions will always remain.

Let me model the image of Christ in all that I do!
Amen.

ROSANN WHITING

"The educational role of the Christian family therefore has a very important place in organic pastoral work. This involves a new form of cooperation between parents and Christian communities, and between the various educational groups and pastors. In this sense, the renewal of the Catholic school must give special attention both to the parents of the pupils and to the formation of a perfect educating community."

FAMILIARIS CONSORTIO §40

1. Recall your favorite school community event from your childhood. What features—people, activities, conversations—made this event so memorable?

2. In what ways have you been successful in forging a home-school connection in your ministry as a Catholic school leader? What successes should be celebrated? What new opportunities await?

3. Christ's message of communion stands in contrast to contemporary society's emphasis on impersonal interaction and communication. How can we as Catholic school leaders, through sharing the gifts of Catholic education with teachers, parents, and students alike, stand as countercultural witnesses to foreground the importance of the Catholic community in an increasingly individualistic age?

PETER CORRIGAN

"Every educator needs a firm hope, because the teacher is never the one who truly reaps the fruits of the labour expended on the students."

LAY CATHOLICS IN SCHOOLS §72

I once taught a religion class to seniors in which one of the students had a condition called Oppositional Defiant Disorder. I had taught this young man in middle school and prayed that he had matured and would not be a problem. Unfortunately, my prayers were in vain because it soon became evident that he would not be cooperating with me during the year.

I racked my brains to come up with some activities, projects, discussion questions that would engage him and his classmates. As is common in this kind of situation, I spent 80% of my time and energy on just 20% of my students. I despaired that any of the students would learn what I was trying to teach them.

One Sunday during Mass, I was again praying for some insight and strength when I heard very clearly, "It's not your job to make them believe. That's my job."

At that moment, I realized that all I could do was teach the best way that I knew how, treat the students—especially this particular one—with compassion and respect, and be open and flexible enough to grab teaching opportunities when they arose. I had to be prepared and creative. But then, I had to trust that God would do the rest.

That moment changed my whole attitude about teaching. It helped me realize that in the end, it is God who does most of the work and ultimately reaps the fruits of my labor. And, you know, that's OK with me.

SISTER BARBARA KANE, O.P.

"Catholic schools must also continue to look for ways to include and serve better the needs of young people in our Church who have special educational and physical needs."

RENEWING OUR COMMITMENT p. 9

Heavenly Father,
Thank You for the gifts and talents You have given me, and for the many ways my actions and interactions can praise and glorify You.

Open my eyes and heart to those in my school who struggle with physical limitations and learning needs.

Help me to treat them as You would, and to welcome them into our school and into our classrooms.

Challenge me to see the mystical body of Christ through their eyes, through their experiences.

Use me as Your advocate for those who are on the fringe and who are marginalized in our Church and school community.

By Your Grace and through my leadership, may this school be a place where all are welcome.
Amen.

ANTHONY HOLTER

"Cultural pluralism, therefore, leads the Church to reaffirm her mission of education to insure strong character formation. Her children, then, will be capable both of resisting the debilitating influence of relativism and of living up to the demands made on them by their Baptism. It also stimulates her to foster truly Christian living and apostolic communities, equipped to make their own positive contribution, in a spirit of cooperation, to the building up of the secular society. For this reason the Church is prompted to mobilize her educational resources in the face of the materialism, pragmatism and technocracy of contemporary society."

THE CATHOLIC SCHOOL §12

---

1. Discuss ways in which your school community can foster "strong character formation" that will allow your students both to resist "the debilitating influence of relativism" and live up to the "demands made on them by their Baptism." What programs do you already have in place to address this formation, and in what areas does your school need to grow?

2. How does your school, in a spirit of cooperation, help to build up the larger community and society of which it is a part?

3. Explain the meaning of the following ideologies and how you see them manifested in the lives of your students and their families: (a) materialism; (b) pragmatism; and (c) technocracy. How can you and your colleagues help to create a positive culture in your school that can help counteract these influences?

SISTER ANNE CATHERINE BURLEIGH, O.P.

"Parents and teachers, your task—and the many conflicts of the present day do not make it an easy one—is to help your children and your students to discover truth, including religious and spiritual truth."

EVANGELII NUNTIANDI §78

---

*I*t is no surprise that the authors call upon parents first in this exhortation. After all, the Church tells us that parents are the first teachers. But they share that responsibility with the schools, so both parent and teacher are given the charge to lead children to truth. In a world that has become increasingly changed by media, where people who have achieved fame have such tremendous affect on our culture, this task is daunting at best. Acquiring celebrity status doesn't qualify a person to lead and shape our young people, yet we find ourselves handing our most impressionable minds and souls over to the pop culture of the day.

The author tells us that this task is difficult. Indeed, the influence of outside culture on our children is so pervasive, it's unlikely that even the most savvy and well-intentioned parent can guard against it. It is for this reason that a family culture rooted in seeking spiritual truth is so critically necessary. Parents must bring this seeking into the fabric of their family life in an intentional and consistent way. The media will be there every single moment of every day. It must be balanced with a strong message at home that the basic teachings of the Church and the search for spiritual truth are the most important messages to hear and act upon. With a strong spiritual foundation, children and adults alike are armed with the ability to sift through the rubble of the day and find the kernel of truth.

Teachers share this difficult task. Catholic educators are given the awesome responsibility of helping parents raise young children to be men and women of faith, integrity, and truth. Developing the spirituality of a young person is a long process that is fraught with challenges. The culture of a school must consistently bring to the forefront the concept of spiritual truth as the only truth that gives life. The mere teaching of religion as a subject is not nearly enough to develop spirituality. Catholic schools create a space for each person to find his or her own relationship with God and in so doing, allow spirituality to be nurtured to maturity.

Parents and teachers must be vigilant in helping students find their core spirituality. It is there that a solid, everlasting relationship with God will be kept safe. With this foundation, a strong young man or woman can interact with the very real influences in today's culture, but still recognize God's truth when they see it.

LORI MOREAU

"If lived authentically and profoundly, the ecclesial dimension of the educational community of the Catholic school cannot be limited to a relationship with the local Christian community. Almost by natural extension, it tends to open onto the horizons of the universal Church."

EDUCATING TOGETHER IN CATHOLIC SCHOOLS §51

1. How does my Catholic school serve its immediate community? How does it serve the world?

2. How can I as a teacher or administrator demonstrate the importance of service to the larger Church to the students, faculty, and parents of my school?

3. How does my school serve the mission of the larger Church?

PATRICK FENNESSY

"For the Word will speak to educators, and remind them of the tremendous greatness of their identity and of their task; Sacramental life will give them the strength they need to live this career, and bring support when they fail; the prayer of the whole Church will present to God, with them and for them, with the assured response that Jesus Christ has promised, all that the human heart desires and pleads for, and even the things that it does not dare to desire or plead for."

LAY CATHOLICS IN SCHOOLS §72

Lord,
Humbly I listen; for guidance, for strength, for confidence. You endlessly provide for me.

Now as You speak, help me to hear and to be led on the path toward fulfilling my task in Your name.

Let me see You in the work I do, and let me work in ways that allow others to see You through my acts.

Thank You for catching me after every fall and providing me strength to fulfill every accomplishment.

You have shown me what I did not think I was able to achieve, and I thank You for being with me as I challenge the limits I have put on myself.

For in this vocation, for today's task and tomorrow's goal, You provide for me the way to selfless acts beyond what is expected.

With hope in my heart and Your communion through sacrament, You inspire me to reach new levels and conquer new challenges.

Lead me to the role where I may do Your will with Your strength, for Your will is my desire, and of my deepest desires only You are aware.

In everlasting thanksgiving and deepest praise, I pray. Amen.

MELISSA REGAN

"The Church has always had a love for its schools, because this is where its children receive their formation."

THE RELIGIOUS DIMENSION OF EDUCATION IN A CATHOLIC SCHOOL §44

Attending my Catholic parish's grade school along with my siblings allowed me to gain an understanding of the Church as a family. I gained a knowledge base from the time I was a young child that has aided me in making decisions and guided me in times of challenge. Understanding the purpose of the Church and appreciating the role of its teachings in my life began at a young age, allowing time for growth and development.

A sincere relationship with God was fostered at an early age, and although reciting prayers was often the norm, as I matured it was very easy to talk to God in a less formal manner. This foundation for prayer was necessary in order for me to reach higher levels in my spiritual life today. Incorporating God and prayer into daily actions has been possible because of my early exposure to a faith-filled life.

Catholic schooling allowed me to build upon a foundation instilled in me by my parents in order to understand my religion more deeply and grow closer to God.

ANNE CHRISTINE BARBERA

"[A Catholic school's] task is fundamentally a synthesis of culture and faith, and a synthesis of faith and life: the first is reached by integrating all the different aspects of human knowledge through the subjects taught, in the light of the Gospel; the second in the growth of the virtues characteristic of the Christian."

THE CATHOLIC SCHOOL §37

---

1. What opportunities does our school provide for teachers to work together, integrating units across different subjects?

2. How are Catholic values and teachings addressed in math, English, science, and social studies?

3. Does the school budget clearly support the stated mission of the school, with proportionate resources for religious education, liturgy, music, the arts, retreat experiences for students and faculty, and faith formation for all?

4. What activities, programs, and resources are the most developmentally appropriate for our students? Which efforts at integrating faith formation with the broader curriculum have been most successful? Which are in need of change?

FATHER RONALD NUZZI

"Of the Catholic school in America we say humbly, and with gratitude for the grace of God manifested in it, that it has nurtured the faith of Jesus Christ in millions of men and women who have lived vibrantly Christian lives and have given themselves generously in service to others."

TO TEACH AS JESUS DID §113

Great and Gracious God,
Thank You
    For Your presence in our schools,
    For the examples of faith You have set before us,
    For blessed individuals who help us find You each day,
    For the many moments of opportunity to share Your
        message with others.
Help us to remember
    That we have Your guidance,
    That no effort goes unnoticed or is unimportant.
Let us learn
    To do little things with great love,
    To watch You transform our seemingly small actions
        into the lifeblood of the Church.
Let us see
    The great history and community of which we are part.
    And You in the small tasks as well as the big.
Amen.

LAURA CASSEL

"By equipping our young people with a sound education, rooted in the Gospel message, the Person of Jesus Christ, and rich in the cherished traditions and liturgical practices of our faith, we ensure that they have the foundation to live morally and uprightly in our complex modern world."

RENEWING OUR COMMITMENT p. 3

---

*T*eaching the brightest boys in the building is often both a blessing and a curse for me. While they are undeniably the best equipped academically to be agents of change in our new global, technological world, they are also often the most skeptical about their own faith and its place in their life. Often the boys who must witness something firsthand to believe, value reason over faith because they have discovered that their own emotions and heart are unreliable at times. Because they are motivated to exercise their brain without my prompting, it has become my mission to exercise their heart as often as I can by keeping them focused on how their vast knowledge and skills might best be used to live out the Gospel message in a modern world that relies on its machines to manage life while marginalizing human interactions.

Moral decision making in a world that often values acquisition over sacrifice can be a difficult and lonely experience. However, teaching students that allowing one's decisions to be guided by the example of Christ, whose love is unchanging and unconditional, can be comforting in a world that changes so quickly. Challenging young men and women to use their knowledge and skills for positive change, reflecting God's command to love one another, and relying on the Church for bolstering that resolve, can steady their life and their workings in a modern world that shifts beneath their feet daily.

SARAH WATSON

"In the sphere of education the Church has a specific role to play. In the light of Tradition and the teaching of the Council, it can be said that it is not only a matter of entrusting the Church with the person's religious and moral education, but of promoting the entire process of the person's education 'together with' the Church.... Certainly, one area in which the family has an irreplaceable role is that of religious education, which enables the family to grow as a 'domestic church.' Religious education and the catechesis of children make the family a true subject of evangelization and the apostle within the Church."

GRATISSIMAM SANE §16

---

1. Is my school a place where all families feel accepted and supported to grow in their faith?

2. Do we truly know the spiritual gifts and needs of the families our school has been called to serve?

3. How do we encourage families to network with the school and each other to strengthen their faith?

4. What do we have to offer our families and what can we learn from them?

5. Do our families recommend us to other families?

AZURE SMILEY

"The lay Catholic educator is a person who exercises a specific mission within the Church by living, in faith, a secular vocation in the communitarian structure of the school: with the best possible professional qualifications, with an apostolic intention inspired by faith, for the integral formation of the human person, in a communication of culture, in an exercise of that pedagogy which will give emphasis to direct and personal contact with students, giving spiritual inspiration to the educational community of which he or she is a member, as well as to all the different persons related to the educational community."

LAY CATHOLICS IN SCHOOL §24

Heavenly Father,
Each day I give myself to my students.
Help me to be attentive to their particular needs.
Let me look deeply into their eyes to understand
    how best I can serve them.
Help me listen with every fiber of my being
    when they seek my guidance.
Make me strong enough to be strong.
Make me compassionate enough to understand
    that failure can be part of successful growth.
Make me mature enough to be consistent
    even when that is not easy to do.
Remind me that my work is never finished,
    for my goal is to help bring them home to you.
Amen.

ROSANN WHITING

"The Catholic school loses its purpose without constant reference to the Gospel and a frequent encounter with Christ. It derives all the energy necessary for its educational work from Him and thus 'creates in the school community an atmosphere permeated with the Gospel spirit of freedom and love.'"

THE CATHOLIC SCHOOL §55

---

*P*erhaps it's the daily grind of administrative tasks that dulls our senses to the grand mission of Catholic education. Overwhelmed by deadlines, often paralyzed by the sheer volume of voicemails, emails and notes, not to mention the increasing demands for accountability in every sector of the educational process, our zeal can grow cold or lukewarm at best. Lukewarm, of course, is not our best. Amidst so many conflicts and difficulties, sometimes we forget that we are a Catholic school or why we're committed to Catholic education. The children can be master teachers during such times of forgetfulness.

It was Faith Day of Catholic Schools' Week, a day which begins with Mass followed by all day Adoration of the Blessed Sacrament. Each class takes its turn to be with Our Lord and to pray especially for our school and families. The assistant principal all but ran down the hallway, rushing in the midst of coordinating the evening Open House and the all-school service assembly that was only minutes from starting. An astute first grade student remarked to no one in particular, "She must be running to see Jesus." He intuitively understood that only going to see Jesus merited running down the school hallway!

Note the depth of his comment. In order to do all of the activities related to school, we must first be with Jesus. Being with Jesus requires silence and time, two very rare commodities today in our noisy and overly busy culture. Today, let us recommit ourselves to Catholic education by committing ourselves to silent prayer time, the reading of Scripture, and frequent reception of the sacraments. Thus fortified and nourished through a deep relationship with Christ, we can truly love those we serve and serve them joyfully.

SISTER JOHN PAUL MYERS, O.P.

75

"This mission demands, from all the members of the educational community, the awareness that educators, as persons and as a community, have an unavoidable responsibility to create an original Christian style. They are required to be witnesses of Jesus Christ and to demonstrate Christian life as bearing light and meaning for everyone."

EDUCATING TOGETHER IN CATHOLIC SCHOOLS §15

1. Why do you think this excerpt uses such strong language—"demands," "unavoidable," and "required"—to convey the responsibilities of creating an original Christian lifestyle?

2. Note as well that the excerpt explains that all members of the educational community must be engaged in this mission. How do you ensure at your school that all are aware of the demands of this mission?

3. In what ways do your students "bear the light" of Christian life? Your faculty? You?

JIM FRABUTT

"It is of the utmost importance that parents exercise their right and obligation toward the younger generation by securing for their children a sound cultural and religious formation. They must also educate them to a deep sense of responsibility in life, especially in such matters as concern the foundation of a family and the procreation and education of children. They must instill in them an unshakable confidence in Divine Providence and a determination to accept the inescapable sacrifices and hardships involved in so noble and important a task as the co-operation with God in the transmitting of human life and the bringing up of children."

MATER ET MAGISTRA §195

Dear Lord,
We thank You for the gift of parents, those special persons who believe in us, support us, and stand up for us. Help them in their role as primary educators of their children.

Help me as I work to support the parents of the children I serve. Give me patience to understand the love and passion that parents feel for their children. Give me guidance as I collaborate with parents to best meet the needs of my students.

Please bless those who do not have parents or whose parents are unable to properly care for them. Let me be a special comfort to these children as I guide them through the school year.
Amen.

PAMELA LYONS

"The school must stimulate the pupil to exercise his intelligence through the dynamics of understanding to attain clarity and inventiveness. It must help him spell out the meaning of his experiences and their truths. Any school which neglects this duty and which offers merely pre-cast conclusions hinders the personal development of its pupils."

THE CATHOLIC SCHOOL §27

How do I stimulate a student's critical thinking ability while imparting knowledge of the Church? The Catholic Church offers the fullness of the Truth, but there is a need in each of us to discover that truth independently. We rely on the Magisterium for guidance and answers; in it we find ourselves and our places. To teach children this absolute truth while stimulating independent thought, to allow "personal development" without offering only "pre-cast conclusions" is a great challenge to teachers and leaders in Catholic schools.

Independent discovery and personal experience are the surest ways for students to internalize new information. The most difficult place to apply this strategy is in the faith formation of our students.

But it is through content areas where our students may find "the meaning of . . . experiences and their truths." True education, the integral formation of Christians, takes place "when young people can relate their study to real-life situations with which they are familiar." Our students may come to better understand God in beauty or science or the Saints.

MICHELLE RYAN

"Let us then pray the Lord of the harvest to send more such workers into the field of Christian education; and let their formation be one of the principal concerns of the pastors of souls and of the superiors of Religious Orders."

DIVINI ILIUS MAGISTRI §88

Lord,
We recognize the need to provide shepherds for our Catholic schools. We pray that Your call will be heard far and wide.

May the hearts of Your chosen be touched and may they respond accordingly. We pray that they will come with open hearts ready to help form the children they will serve.

We are grateful for Your guiding hand. We pray that our spiritual leaders will be filled with wisdom. May they know the needs of our Catholic educators and share their spiritual gifts with them.

We pray in turn that these gifts will be shared with students who come to us for spiritual nourishment.
Amen.

LORI MOREAU

"To organize schools like gymnasiums where one exercises to establish positive relationships between the various members and to search for peaceful solutions to the conflicts is a fundamental objective not just for the life of the educational community, but also for the construction of a society of peace and harmony."

CONSECRATED PERSONS AND THEIR MISSION IN SCHOOLS §43

Loving God,
Thank You for calling me to the ministry of leadership. I recognize that my role is to create a community with the staff at the school—teachers, secretaries, custodians, and all who contribute to the educational ministry.

I recognize that there are times of disagreement and conflict among these individuals. Let me be the instrument of peace and justice in dealing with these individuals.

This is not easy because of the multiple tasks that I am involved in, but slow me down, helping me to see the goodness in each of these individuals.

Let me model the peace-filled message of Jesus. Let this community of committed individuals be a witness to You and the values that Jesus taught us during His life on earth.

We ask this in Jesus' name.
Amen.

SISTER MARY JANE HERB, I.H.M.

"A Catholic school is not simply a place where lessons are taught; it is a center that has an operative educational philosophy, attentive to the needs of today's youth and illumined by the Gospel message."

THE RELIGIOUS DIMENSION OF EDUCATION IN A CATHOLIC SCHOOL §22

---

1. How would you express your school's educational philosophy?

2. Is your school attentive to the needs of youth in your community? How does your school particularly respond to these needs?

3. How does the Gospel influence your response to the needs of your community?

4. How can you contribute to shaping your school's educational philosophy?

5. How can you ensure that the Gospel positively influences the way you respond to the needs of young people?

DAN TULLY

"Thus the Catholic school should be able to offer young people the means to acquire the knowledge they need in order to find a place in a society which is strongly characterized by technical and scientific skill. But at the same time, it should be able, above all, to impart a solid Christian formation."

THE CATHOLIC SCHOOL ON THE THRESHOLD OF THE THIRD MILLENNIUM §8

While in Catholic school, my school code referred to my school as the training ground where I must mold myself into a "useful man." When you think of training ground, what are your first thoughts? Of course, the basics are important for any school—math, science, English, and social studies classes, among others. But what sets Catholic schools apart from all other schools is the unique opportunity for students to truly learn the importance of being a Christian. It brings education to the personal level.

Albert Einstein once said, "Education is what remains after one has forgotten what one has learned in school." The education that one receives in a Catholic school goes beyond any knowledge one can report in terms of test scores and grades. It includes the fostering of Christian and Catholic ideals of faith, hope, and love and provides an example of the everlasting impact Christian beliefs can have on one's life.

As a Catholic school teacher or leader, you are that example and you are the reason why so many students receive more in school than how to say their ABCs or how to find the derivative of something. Continually reflect on your role and how you can improve it, relying on your own Christian formation and belief. The Lord called you to this role for a reason and He still works within you that you may fulfill that role effectively. Be open to His love and support and pass it on to all those you impact in your school.

KEVIN KIMBERLY

"Knowledge is not to be considered as a means of material prosperity and success, but as a call to serve and to be responsible for others."

THE CATHOLIC SCHOOL §56

Dear Lord,
We pray for safety and peace for all our children, especially those touched by our current immigration issues.

We pray for the love and wisdom to show complete acceptance for each child within our school and classrooms.

Father, guide us in modeling and becoming a living example of the body of Christ in all our interactions with our students and their families.

Guide us in becoming the Catholic educational community we are charged with being.

We ask this through Christ our Lord.
Amen.

KATHY ASMAR

"The first requirement, then, for a lay educator who wishes to live out his or her ecclesial vocation, is the acquisition of a solid professional formation. In the case of an educator, this includes competency in a wide range of cultural, psychological, and pedagogical areas."

LAY CATHOLICS IN SCHOOLS §27

Too often *vocation* and *professional formation* are viewed as contradictory, distinct, or at best complementary. In truth, vocation and formation depend on each other, both enlivened by the grace-filled interplay between God's gifts and human development of those gifts.

From one perspective, vocation is interpreted as a "call" to a role in life. From another perspective, vocation is an expression of oneself. One's life work or vocation expresses and continually develops one's given talents, skills, and interests in a way that is consistent with God's creative plan for the world. The Holy Spirit gives lay educators gifts of personal faith, intellectual curiosity, patience, charisma, courage, and deep wells of love for others that are beautifully expressed through their roles in Catholic schools. But these gifts are not enough. These spiritual gifts need to be prepared and continually fostered within a framework that synthesizes all the different elements that make Catholic school educators great. This is professional formation at its best.

Good professional formation refines and amplifies one's inherent giftedness or vocation. This is natural, and it is graced. Lay educators have a natural desire to always increase their academic knowledge base, expand their foundation of educational pedagogy, and explore how people learn and grow. Professional formation guides the human desire to develop, and it is graced because God infuses our human response to those desires when they are cultivated and expanded in service of God's Kingdom.

MAX ENGEL

"No Christian education can be considered complete unless it covers every kind of obligation. It must therefore aim at implanting and fostering among the faithful an awareness of their duty to carry on their economic and social activities in a Christian manner."

MATER ET MAGISTRA §228

---

1. How can we as educators emphasize the importance of incorporating Christian works into all aspects of our students' lives? How does our faculty model this mission in our school, and how can we provide more comprehensive examples for our students?

2. How does our school frame the inclusion of Christian actions in our subject curriculum? Do students understand that God is present in everything, including schoolwork?

3. What opportunities does our school provide for students to live out their social and economic obligations?

ANNE CHRISTINE BARBERA

"In a Catholic school, everyone should be aware of the living presence of Jesus the 'Master' who, today as always is with us in our journey through life as the one genuine 'Teacher', the perfect Man in whom all human values find their fullest perfection. The inspiration of Jesus must be translated from the ideal into the real. The Gospel spirit should be evident in a Christian way of thought and life which permeates all facets of the educational climate."

THE RELIGIOUS DIMENSION OF EDUCATION IN A CATHOLIC SCHOOL §25

Lord God,
We are grateful for the dedicated men and women
    that serve as Catholic educators.
They make tremendous personal sacrifices
    to carry out the mission of Your Church.

Lord, bless them with:
    Strength when they are weak;
    Encouragement when they are discouraged;
    Spirit when they are frustrated;
    And joy when they need it most.

Our religious and lay professionals
    define our institutions through their words and deeds.
Allow them to represent Your will
    as it should be represented.

We ask this through Jesus Christ, our Lord.
Amen.

CHRISTOPHER BOTT

"The ecclesial nature of the Catholic school, therefore, is written in the very heart of its identity as a teaching institution. It is a true and proper ecclesial entity by reason of its educational activity, 'in which faith, culture and life are brought into harmony.'"

THE CATHOLIC SCHOOL ON THE THRESHOLD OF THE THIRD MILLENNIUM §11

---

*I*n a Catholic school, we cannot separate faith or Catholic identity from the academic program. Without providing students with faith formation or spiritual development, the education would be incomplete. However, knowing that students of various religious and cultural backgrounds choose Catholic schools, how do we attend to the mission of the Church while serving such a wide range of students?

I keep in mind that a former archbishop once made a remark to the effect that we do not serve because our students are Catholic but because we are Catholic. It is in this spirit that while we spread our faith, we celebrate the differences among those in our community—differences in talent, ethnicity, and personality. We work with these differences and learn from these differences so that our school community grows together and creates a rich tapestry of life.

With the close support of the parish, the constant presence of the clergy, the weekly attendance at school Mass, and involvement in the activities surrounding the liturgical seasons, our students share in the traditions of the Church. They learn how the tenets of the faith are of value in helping them to grow into caring, responsible citizens. They learn not only to appreciate people from all walks of life, but how to be of service to others as well.

The integration of faith, culture, and life with our academic program provides our students with a strong foundation of knowledge, a deep sense of morality, and the desire to lead as conscientious citizens who strive for the common good of society.

JENNIFER KETCHUM

"A Catholic school cannot relinquish its own freedom to proclaim the Gospel and to offer a formation based on the values to be found in a Christian education; this is its right and its duty."

THE RELIGIOUS DIMENSION OF EDUCATION IN A CATHOLIC SCHOOL §6

1. Who are the students and families I have failed? What do they have in common?

2. What would they say about me? Did I push them to grow? Did I give them the tools they will need to do God's work in their church, family, and community? Did I listen to them? Did I believe in them?

3. Did I guide them toward a deeper understanding of self through God? Are they better Christians because of their time with me? How can my experiences with these students and families provide me an opportunity to serve the Lord in more effective ways in the future?

AZURE SMILEY

"The proper and immediate end of Christian education is to cooperate with divine grace in forming the true and perfect Christian, that is, to form Christ Himself in those regenerated by Baptism."

DIVINI ILIUS MAGISTRI §94

Dear Loving Father,
I am so very blessed. I thank You for bringing me to this position in Catholic education where my mission is clear.

You ask me to "cooperate with divine grace." Your request seems so simple, yet it is so very difficult to achieve. How is it possible for one as flawed as me to help build such a "true and perfect Christian" from among Your disciples?

Only through Your perfect grace is this even possible. In Your infinite wisdom You made each of us to have our own will. Help me to relinquish my yearnings for control and let You work through me, revealing to these young people what Your will is for them.

Your wish for me is to guide these young people to accept Christ as their entire life—their will, focus, and desire. Place in my heart a will to accept this myself so that I can feel You move within me. Especially as I work with these young people, be ever present in my mind, on my lips, and in my heart.

Ever aware of my need for You,
I ask this through Your Son, Jesus.
Amen.

HEATHER LINDSAY

"One crucial measure of the success or failure of the educational ministry is how well it enables men to hear the message of hope contained in the Gospel, to base their love and service of God upon this message, to achieve a vital personal relationship with Christ, and to share the Gospel's realistic view of the human condition which recognizes the fact of evil and personal sin while affirming hope."

TO TEACH AS JESUS DID §8

The motto of my religious community, the Congregation of Holy Cross, is *Crux Spes Unica,* "The Cross, Our Only Hope." Our constitutions note that as educators in the faith, we must be men with "hope to bring." For me, proclaiming hope or enabling students to hear the Gospel message of hope means cultivating an attitude of *promise,* that is, affirming for each student the reality of *possibility, expectation,* and *aspiration.*

Possibility means recognizing that every student has potential and working with each student to make that potential a reality. Every teacher needs to believe and help every student to understand that by God's grace he or she can learn, has talents, and has an important contribution to make to society.

Expectation implies that a Catholic school has high but realistic expectations of students and enables students to have high and realistic expectations of themselves. American culture creates an expectation of instant gratification and entitlement, and defines success in terms of wealth, pleasure, and power. A Catholic school creates an expectation of growth and defines success as a virtuous life well-lived for others.

Aspiration proposes setting high goals. Students need to be inspired to do great things, and to grow in virtue, wisdom, and knowledge. A Catholic school is in the "business" of forming saints. As Robert Browning said, "A man's reach should exceed his grasp or what's a heaven for?"

Hope is the inner conviction based on faith that God will provide for us and through us. It is a virtue of the Holy Spirit that needs to permeate the culture of every Catholic school.

BROTHER WILLIAM DYGERT, C.S.C.

"Prime responsibility for creating this unique Christian school climate rests with the teachers, as individuals and as a community. The religious dimension of the school climate is expressed through the celebration of Christian values in Word and Sacrament, in individual behavior, in friendly and harmonious interpersonal relationships, and in a ready availability. Through this daily witness, the students will come to appreciate the uniqueness of the environment to which their youth has been entrusted. If it is not present, then there is little left which can make the school Catholic."

THE RELIGIOUS DIMENSION OF EDUCATION IN A CATHOLIC SCHOOL §26

1. Do I live up to all Christian values in word, sacrament, and individual behavior in both my work and personal life?

2. What daily witness can I bring to my classroom in order to create a "unique Christian school climate"?

3. How can I encourage my students to value their youth and education, ensuring that they appreciate the uniqueness of their environment?

CHRISTIE HJERPE

"Above all the education of youth from every social background has to be undertaken, so that there can be produced not only men and women of refined talents, but those great-souled persons who are so desperately required by our times."

GAUDIUM ET SPES §31

Lord Jesus,
Before Your ascension You said, "Go, therefore, and make disciples of all nations" (Mt 28:19).

Your mandate continues to inspire and encourage educators to teach the truth of the dignity of each person, created in Your image and likeness. To You, there are no distinctions between cultures, languages, social standing.

You alone know the hearts of us all, and You desire to penetrate our hearts and draw them close to You. To follow You, to be Your disciple, is to know who and whose we are. You alone satisfy the deepest desires of the human heart for happiness.

May we who are entrusted with the noble task of educating young people see the indwelling of the Holy Spirit in the depths of each student's soul.

May young people of every time and place grow in the knowledge of You and respond generously to Your call to holiness of life.
Amen.

SISTER JOHN PAUL MYERS, O.P.

"In spite of numerous obstacles, the Catholic school has continued to share responsibility for the social and cultural development of the different communities and peoples to which it belongs, participating in their joys and hopes, their sufferings and difficulties, their efforts to achieve genuine human and communitarian progress."

THE CATHOLIC SCHOOL ON THE THRESHOLD OF THE THIRD MILLENNIUM §5

The crowded cafeteria looks a bit odd on this special day. Approximately 150 elderly people sit at the tables that are normally reserved for hundreds of Catholic school students. About three dozen students, teachers, administrators, and community leaders hurry to prepare the meals, serve them, and leave a few minutes to chat with the guests.

A student sits in the back of the cafeteria playing a piano that is in desperate need of tuning. The music sounds like something from the 1950s and the guests sway back and forth in their seats with the beat of the music. The tone of the room is busy and happy. I stop at a table to witness a man, probably in his late eighties, telling a joke to three of our freshman boys. He gets to the punch line and laughs hysterically with the students, as he pounds his open hand on the table. The students' laughter is genuine and I can tell that they are enjoying themselves.

I move on to witness one of our junior students holding the hand of a woman who is visibly upset. The student assures her that everything is going to be okay and that she is there to help her.

The inhabitants of the local nursing home visit our school every Palm Sunday to break bread and enjoy the company of our school community members. Our intentions in beginning the tradition focused mostly on helping others. As I walk through the room on these special days and see the interaction between the two communities, I wonder about our students' perspective of this event. I ask myself in the silence of my mind, "Who is the true beneficiary of this gathering?"

CHRISTOPHER BOTT

"Apart from their theological formation, educators need also to cultivate their spiritual formation in order to develop their relationship with Jesus Christ and become a Master like Him."

EDUCATING TOGETHER IN CATHOLIC SCHOOLS §26

1. How often do I practice the prayers and meditative, spiritual exercises that I teach to my students? Can I commit to sharing with my students one new spiritual practice a month? What would it look like if the whole school committed to such an exercise?

2. What are some ways that I can make spiritual formation a bigger priority in my life? Can I seek the counsel of a spiritual advisor? What if I reach out to my colleagues to form or join a prayer group? What areas of my personal spirituality need to be recharged or renewed?

3. How does the celebration of the Eucharist on Sunday impact my work and ministry at the school during the week? What might I do differently at church or at school to make that important connection more salient? How does my personal prayer life inspire and shape my role as spiritual leader in the school?

ANTHONY HOLTER

"Catholic school personnel should be grounded in a faith-based Catholic culture, have strong bonds to Christ and the Church, and be witnesses to the faith in both their words and actions. The formation of personnel will allow the Gospel message and the living presence of Jesus to permeate the entire life of the school community and thus be faithful to the school's evangelizing mission."

RENEWING OUR COMMITMENT p. 9

Make us vessels
who convey the Catholic faith by word and example...
Lord, we pray.

Bind us, God,
to Your Son, Jesus Christ, and Your mother Church...
Lord, we pray.

Create in us
a strong Christian foundation...
Lord, we pray.

Help us
to live out Your Gospel message throughout our school day...
Lord, we pray.

Nourish us
with the living presence of Jesus...
Lord, we pray.

And make us faithful servants
who help You, Lord, to gather the lost sheep...
Lord, we pray.

LORI MOREAU

"No less than other schools does the Catholic school pursue cultural goals and the human formation of youth. But its proper function is to create for the school community a special atmosphere animated by the Gospel spirit of freedom and charity, to help youth grow according to the new creatures they were made through baptism as they develop their own personalities, and finally to order the whole of human culture to the news of salvation so that the knowledge the students gradually acquire of the world, life and man is illumined by faith."

GRAVISSIMUM EDUCATIONIS §8

---

*G*rowing up attending a Catholic elementary school in Cincinnati, Ohio, my Lenten experience quickly became associated with one event: Fish Fry Fridays! My love of Lenten Fridays was not because I loved fried perch (sometimes I opted for the cheese pizza instead), but rather because these were nights when the whole parish and school community came together. Teachers, parishioners, and fellow classmates made these nights memorable.

When I moved to Tucson, Arizona, to begin my first year teaching at Santa Cruz Catholic School through Notre Dame's ACE Program, I looked forward to a similar Lenten community experience. After I became aware that the parish community did not have any plans for a fish fry, I began discussing possibilities with my eighth grade class. What if, we brainstormed, the eighth grade led a Lenten almsgiving project?

When discussing possible charities, I introduced the class to Heifer International, a justice organization that promotes economic development for poor farmers in the developing world. The class loved this idea and developed a three-pronged set of projects to meet this goal: two fish fry nights, a car wash, and a junior high dance.

While all the projects were successful, the fish fry nights proved to be exceptional. The school, parish, and larger community all gathered in great numbers to share a meal.

I was overwhelmed with gratitude for the spirit of generosity that the students showed as they worked to raise several thousand dollars for Heifer. The "true spirit of the Church" was palpably present in these student-driven experiences of service and community.

PETER CORRIGAN

"Independent research on Catholic schools consistently points to their success in educating students to the highest standards of scholarship and moral and social responsibility, often under pressing economic conditions."

PRINCIPLES FOR EDUCATIONAL REFORM IN THE UNITED STATES p. 2

1. What are the ways in which my school defines success?

2. Do I try to develop my students morally as well as intellectually?

3. How do I exhibit the lessons I want my students to learn?

4. Do I consistently exemplify the Catholic faith I teach in both my words and my actions?

5. What are the obstacles that impede the ideals I hold for my students?

LAURA CASSEL

"A school is not only a place where one is given a choice of intellectual values, but a place where one has presented an array of values which are actively lived. The school must be a community whose values are communicated through the interpersonal and sincere relationships of its members and through both individual and corporative adherence to the outlook on life that permeates the school."

THE CATHOLIC SCHOOL §32

Giving Lord,
Our Catholic schools have enjoyed a rich history
of supporting the communities they belong to.

Allow us to continue in this tradition of Your work,
    To feed the hungry,
    Console the suffering,
    Clothe the naked,
    Shelter the homeless,
    And befriend the lonely.

Let these mutually beneficial relationships
remain as a focal point of our schools.

We ask this through Christ, our Lord.
Amen.

CHRISTOPHER BOTT

"Christian education is intended to 'make men's faith become living, conscious, and active, through the light of instruction.' The Catholic school is the unique setting within which this ideal can be realized in the lives of Catholic children and young people."

TO TEACH AS JESUS DID §102

---

*O*ur days are filled with curriculum, lesson plans, and assessments. Sometimes it seems that the faith aspect of the school is separate, though equally important. But these are not separate goals. All our work is the conduit to God.

During an afternoon English lesson, an eighth grader responded to something I said with, "Why does everything here have to be so Catholic?"

I reminded him that this is a Catholic school.

"Yeah, but we're in English class."

I read and discussed the school mission statement with the class. We talked about the idea that everything we do is meant to bring us closer to God, and that school is where we learn about our talents and preferences and discern our vocation. The ultimate goal is not just to graduate; it is the complete integration of Christian formation in the minds and hearts of students. It is to help build the Kingdom of God and to share eternal life with our Lord.

Each of us, at times, needs to be reminded of our intention in Christian education. The potential to lose sight of our eternal mission is a danger to all members of the school community: teachers, parents, children. It is at these times that school leaders are so crucial to bringing the mission of the school back into focus.

MICHELLE RYAN

"The role of evangelization is precisely to educate people in the faith in such a way as to lead each individual Christian to live the sacraments as true sacraments of faith—and not to receive them passively or reluctantly."

EVANGELII NUNTIANDI §47

Lord Jesus,
You are the source of all life, of all that is true, good, and beautiful.

In Your great love and mercy, You give us a share in Your very life through the gift of the sacraments. The sacraments have the power to sustain and nourish us as they impart to each of us the life of grace.

Often we fail to be attentive to Your Presence, especially in the Eucharist. We are distracted by our own pursuits, our busyness, and the constant hum of activity around us.

May we settle our souls so that we may be attentive to You as You come to each of us personally.

May the fire of the Holy Spirit fill our hearts, inspiring us to seek You. In seeking You, may we come to know You.

In knowing You, may we desire to touch You and be touched by You in the sacraments.
Amen.

SISTER JOHN PAUL MYERS, O.P.

"Educators must be welcoming and well-prepared interlocutors, able to awaken and direct the best energies of students towards the search for truth and the meaning of existence, a positive construction of themselves and of life in view of an overall formation."

EDUCATING TOGETHER IN CATHOLIC SCHOOLS §2

1. What attitudes and habits do you cultivate that foster your own search for truth and the meaning of existence?

2. How do you maintain a balance in communicating to others—students and colleagues—that you are seeking truth, while also serving as a knowledgeable guide and authority figure in the classroom or school?

3. Within a conversation, how do you respond to disagreement? Are you someone that avoids it at all costs? Seeks it?

4. What is a person's "overall formation" and what do Catholic schools have to do with this process?

MAX ENGEL

"The community aspect of the Catholic school is necessary because of the nature of the faith and not simply because of the nature of man and the nature of the educational process which is common to every school. No Catholic school can adequately fulfill its educational role on its own."

THE CATHOLIC SCHOOL §54

Sometimes it is really hard to get out of bed on Sunday morning and go to church. We put our whole hearts into our calling as educators which leaves little time for rest and relaxation. Often, on Sunday morning I lay in bed and wonder "why can't I just stay in bed and pray by myself?" We go to church so we can pray together and belong to the larger Catholic community. We are many parts, but all one body of Christ.

While abroad in Rome, I attended Easter Mass in Saint Peter's Square with Pope Benedict XVI. In addition to being blessed by the Holy Father's presence, 150 friends from my Catholic university were by my side, having traveled from all over Europe to celebrate Christ's resurrection in the holiest of cities. Together, we were the body of Christ for our school and for our Church. We were united in love for Jesus and for each other that freezing morning in our Easter dresses. Never in my life had I felt closer to God. Here we were, 5,000 miles from home, with 15,000 strangers, yet we were all one, hanging on every word, in every language, that came out of Pope Benedict's mouth. You can't teach people to feel like they belong. They have to want to belong, have to believe, and have to experience God's call firsthand. Every Catholic school should foster such community. There is no other community as great as a Catholic school. Every child should feel as if they're in Saint Peter's Square every day in our classrooms.

Our vocation as Catholic educators calls us to love every student that enters our classroom. Not only do we need to love our students, but parents, faculty, staff, and all others belonging to the school community. The first thing I tell my children is: You are loved. You will be loved by me and this community, for this year, and every year hereafter. This is a direct result of Jesus' love for us. Christ shines through you and me and encourages us to love each other. We are a part of this larger community every day in spirit, word, and action.

Jesus himself called us to be a messenger to students. By establishing community within our schools, we must feel confident that Jesus will speak through us; we are his lips, hands, and feet. The community of the Catholic school is what sets it apart from all other options: an education is not complete without faith, hope, and love.

CHRISTIE HJERPE

"The educational mission of the Church is an integrated ministry embracing three interlocking dimensions: the message revealed by God (didache) which the Church proclaims; fellowship in the life of the Holy Spirit (koinonia); service to the Christian community and the entire human community (diakonia)."

TO TEACH AS JESUS DID §14

1. Reflecting on your own school community, in what ways is each dimension—*didache, koinonia,* and *diakonia*—made manifest?

2. Which dimension does your school embrace most strongly? Which dimension presents the greatest opportunity for growth?

3. List and describe two or three concrete steps that your school could take to more fully support the integrated dimensions of Catholic education.

JIM FRABUTT

"Not a few young people, unable to find any meaning in life or trying to find an escape from loneliness, turn to alcohol drugs, the erotic, the exotic, etc. Christian education is faced with the huge challenge of helping these young people discover something of value in their lives."

THE RELIGIOUS DIMENSION OF EDUCATION IN A CATHOLIC SCHOOL §13

Heavenly Father,
You knew me in my mother's womb;
Help me to know Your plan for my life today.

You knew me as a child;
Help me to grow evermore in Your love.

You know me now;
Help me to live so that my students may come to know You.
Amen.

ANTHONY HOLTER

"Christian education takes in the whole aggregate of human life, physical and spiritual, intellectual and moral, individual, domestic and social, not with a view of reducing it in any way, but in order to elevate, regulate, and perfect it, in accordance with the example and teaching of Christ."

DIVINI ILIUS MAGISTRI §95

How do we define a human life? Is it measured by a person's monetary success? The number of friends they have? The lines of accomplishment that fill a resume?

So often we get caught up in these miniscule representations of what a human life is that we fail to see the big picture. We reduce ourselves to an occupation, a statistic, or a title, when the whole aggregate of human life is so much more.

In my life as a student I have struggled to define myself apart from the grades I receive. I have found that the best teachers are those who can inspire growth not only in the classroom, but outside of it as well. These individuals are the ones who can expand the vision of their students to see themselves in a new, more dynamic way. Instead of pigeonholing students by their academic accomplishments, these teachers use the classroom material to expand the worldview of their students and build upon their already existing strengths.

The world is not a series of isolated environments but an integrated whole. The mission of Catholic schools should reflect this dynamism with an eye to every part of the individual. In my own experience, my seventh grade teacher was the one who recognized my strengths not only academically, but athletically as well. With her encouragement, I pursued running as a sport, something that has come to greatly enrich my perspective both as a student and a Christian.

LAURA CASSEL

"And so, now as in the past, the Catholic school must be able to speak for itself effectively and convincingly. It is not merely a question of adaptation, but of missionary thrust, the fundamental duty to evangelize, to go towards men and women wherever they are, so that they may receive the gift of salvation."

THE CATHOLIC SCHOOL ON THE THRESHOLD OF THE THIRD MILLENNIUM §3

In a time when the future of Catholic schools in the United States is threatened more than ever, Catholic school leaders must always be able to present a compelling case for Catholic education, communicating a vision to their communities that is grounded in the Church's understanding of her mission. Imagine you are in a discussion with a Catholic who is not fully convinced of the need for Catholic education. Consider how you would respond to the following objections:

1. "Catholic education, although a great idea in theory, is more expensive and not as relevant as other opportunities for evangelization in the Church today."

2. "At our local grade school, the kids don't even know their faith and their behavior is the same as the kids at the public school. I don't know why I should pay for an education that isn't truly Catholic."

3. "I think we as a Catholic school have no business accepting non-Catholics who don't even share our faith."

4. "How are you supposed to keep a school Catholic when you don't have any sisters or priests teaching anymore?"

SISTER ANNE CATHERINE BURLEIGH, O.P.

"The educational program should help students develop to the fullest, their physical, social, spiritual, moral, and intellectual qualities."

PRINCIPLES FOR EDUCATIONAL REFORM IN THE UNITED STATES p. 5

Lord,
May our students treat their bodies with respect and care.

May they establish strong and lasting relationships with others, finding You in them.

May they embrace solitude, a life of prayer, and find ways to express their faith through service.

May they make decisions that respect life, uphold the dignity of all persons, and support the common good.

May they think critically, be imaginative, and enrich their minds through knowledge and discovery.

Guide them as they grow on all these levels, reaching their full human potential imparted by Your creation.
Amen.

JIM FRABUTT

"The teacher under discussion here is not simply a professional person who systematically transmits a body of knowledge in the context of a school; 'teacher' is to be understood as 'educator'—one who helps to form human persons. The task of a teacher goes well beyond transmission of knowledge, although that is not excluded."

LAY CATHOLICS IN SCHOOLS §16

---

*J*t's easy, especially in a Catholic, college preparatory high school, to get caught up in how many students go on to college, or how many merit scholarships are awarded. These data are important, for sure. Indeed, everything that goes on at a Catholic school should be excellent.

But sometimes we lose sight of what is the most important about our schools: preparing well-formed students who serve the world around them.

There was a student a few years back at my school who didn't seem to fit the mold of a typical high school student. Her peers were nice to her, but she didn't seem to have a real group of friends. Regardless, she'd lead the school in prayer once a week, offering profound reflections on the Gospel and how it related to her life. And the students listened to her.

After graduation, I was told that she would not have graduated were it not for significant accommodations, well outside of those the school normally offered. All along, her parents told the administrators and counselors that they didn't care if she went to college; they just wanted her to be in a Catholic school where she could express her deep, powerful faith.

Her teachers could have written her off, but they met her where she was and embraced the gifts that she brought the school, even if they weren't academic gifts. They realized that while she might not be the top student in their classes, she was a special person with something to give to others.

This student still comes to school often. She visits her old teachers, helps with PE classes, and writes encouraging letters to people going on retreats. She didn't go to college or earn a merit scholarship, but she is probably one of the best examples of what we want our graduates to be: people of deep faith who selflessly serve the Church.

PATRICK FENNESSY

"By their witness and their behavior teachers are of the first importance to impart a distinctive character to Catholic schools."

THE CATHOLIC SCHOOL §78

---

1. As a school leader, how can I support my faculty during those trying times of the year? How does my leadership style model the behaviors I wish to see in my teachers?

2. As a school leader, how can I attract the kind of teachers who will be dynamic leaders in the classroom as well as with their peers?

3. As a school leader, how can I bring parents and teachers together in a collegial manner so that all of our decisions benefit the students entrusted to our care?

ROSANN WHITING

"Our young people are the Church of today and tomorrow. It is imperative that we provide them with schools ready to address their spiritual, moral, and academic needs."

RENEWING OUR COMMITMENT p. 8

Dear Jesus,
Help us to treasure the young people You have entrusted to our care. In them we see hope for the future of the Church and the world.

Give us the grace to be teachers after Your own heart. May we be compassionate with the struggling and patient with the wayward. May we inspire courage in the timid and zeal in the lukewarm.

Help us always to be truthful in our words and challenging in our expectations. Grant us the grace to present the power of the Gospel in all of its compelling beauty.

Help us strive to bring glory to Your name by being always conscientious in our preparations, remembering that we reveal the dignity of work through attention to the daily details.

Lord Jesus, give us strength to be witnesses to You. May our every word, our every glance, our every action reflect the love we have for You, poured out on Your children. Amen.

SISTER ANNE CATHERINE BURLEIGH, O.P.

"The Catholic teacher, therefore, cannot be content simply to present Christian values as a set of abstract objectives to be admired, even if this be done positively and with imagination; they must be presented as values which generate human attitudes, and these attitudes must be encouraged in the students."

LAY CATHOLICS IN SCHOOLS §30

The questions continued to resurface in my head. How could I possibly ask this student to leave our school at the conclusion of her junior year? During the three years she had been with us she had excelled in many areas. Her performance in the classroom was exceptional, she participated in athletics and the band, was universally respected throughout our building, and was a genuinely good person. Was it her fault that her parents fell on difficult financial times? The practical administrator side of my brain decided to interfere. What about the rules? Is it fair to everyone else if you let her slide? My level of frustration increased and I decided to take a walk through the building to settle down.

I dropped into several classrooms and observed a great mixture of activities, teaching, and learning that put a smile on my face. I found a teacher grading papers during a free period and decided to stop in and say hello. The teacher was several months pregnant and was showing signs of being tired from the demands of the day.

As I entered the room she looked up at me and smiled. She then said, "I know that this is none of my business, but I heard that Mary's parents are experiencing financial trouble and that she may not return for her senior year. I have talked it over with my husband and we would like to cover the difference between her tuition cost and what her parents can afford."

I must have been staring at her belly and she caught me. She laughed and said, "I know, but we can put it on a credit card and deal with it later."

I thanked her, indicated that I would get back to her once I had more information, and walked out of the room more confused than ever.

CHRISTOPHER BOTT

"A Christian education does not merely strive for the maturing of a human person . . . but has as its principal purpose this goal: that the baptized, while they are gradually introduced to the knowledge of the mystery of salvation, become ever more aware of the gift of Faith they have received, and that they learn in addition how to worship God the Father in spirit and truth (cf. John 4:23) especially in liturgical action, and be conformed in their personal lives according to the new man created in justice and holiness of truth (Eph. 4:22-24); also that they develop into perfect manhood, to the mature measure of the fullness of Christ (cf. Eph. 4:13) and strive for the growth of the Mystical Body; moreover, that aware of their calling, they learn not only how to bear witness to the hope that is in them (cf. Peter 3:15) but also how to help in the Christian formation of the world that takes place when natural powers viewed in the full consideration of man redeemed by Christ contribute to the good of the whole society."

GRAVISSIMUM EDUCATIONIS §2

God of all goodness,
Source of love and giver of all good gifts, in Your divine plan, You gave Your Son Jesus a blessed and holy mother.

Gracious Mother Mary,
Like you love your Son, Jesus, you love each of us and want to see us grow to become the people God created us to be.

My role as an educator is a challenging one. In my thankfulness for all that God's gift of salvation has given me, I often try to help students see the power of this gift.

God often reveals to me that they may not be ready for all that this gift entails. God asks me to help students recognize the gift of faith that has been instilled in them. If they are able to recognize their own gift of faith, they will experience God through the liturgy, conform their own will to God's, and work to strengthen the Church through their witness.

These important stepping stones are so far apart though. How do I help students make the gigantic leaps between them?

Mother Mary, help me to guide the students, as you guided your Son. Help me to give them worthy directions and guide them to stay in the path of light. It may be through your intercession that God will be able to guide my faltering instructions into a straight way through the desert of life.

In union with all the Saints and in Jesus' name I pray. Amen.

HEATHER LINDSAY

"By its very nature, the Catholic school requires the presence and involvement of educators that are not only culturally and spiritually formed, but also intentionally directed at developing their community educational commitment in an authentic spirit of ecclesial communion."

EDUCATING TOGETHER IN CATHOLIC SCHOOLS §34

1. What is an "authentic spirit of ecclesial communion"?

2. How can one tell if such an authentic spirit exists in an educational community?

3. What types of staff development opportunities would support cultural and spiritual formation in a newly hired Catholic school teacher?

LORI MOREAU

"Education in the Catholic school, therefore, through the tools of teaching and learning, 'is not given for the purpose of gaining power but as an aid towards a fuller understanding of, and communion with man, events and things.' This principle affects every scholastic activity, the teaching and even all the after-school activities such as sport, theatre and commitment in social work, which promote the creative contribution of the students and their socialization."

EDUCATING TOGETHER IN CATHOLIC SCHOOLS §39

*J*t is commonly accepted wisdom today that Catholic schools are not well prepared for the task of marketing themselves. Professional organizations have come to the rescue, offering workshops, classes, public relations personnel, national campaigns, and slick advertisements to get the word out: Catholic schools are good schools, often surpassing their public school counterparts on similar measures of achievement.

A popular ad campaign occurs every spring near graduation time when Catholic high schools take out large, paid advertisements in the secular and Catholic press to announce the university selections of each of their graduates. Frequently these announcements also contain a listing of the dollar amount of scholarships earned or offered to each graduate and, as a leading title, the total amount of scholarships earned by the graduating class.

We are right to be proud of Catholic school success and such celebration of our graduates is a strategic and thoughtful way to market the benefits of a Catholic school education. But one does not embrace the faith for money, nor do parents sacrifice for their children for the singular purpose of earning scholarships for college. The academic pursuits of a Catholic school education—or any education—will only take you so far. Academic excellence is not a Gospel value.

It would be refreshing, during some future spring, if a Catholic school celebrated its graduates' successes by telling the world about their commitment to service, their hours invested ministering with the poor, their advocacy on behalf of justice, their efforts to transform the community and enrich the local church. It would be an evangelical joy to read about all the activities that helped shape their resumés into Christ-like testimonies and their hearts into Christian disciples. Being on the way to college is a good thing, but being on the road to the Kingdom is even better.

FATHER RONALD NUZZI

"The entire effort of the Catholic teacher is oriented toward an integral formation of each student."

LAY CATHOLICS IN SCHOOLS §28

1. Have I given my whole self to my vocation as a teacher?

2. Do I take time to focus on the development of each individual in my classroom, concentrating on his or her unique needs and gifts?

3. What lessons are necessary for the holistic formation of my students?

4. What kind of people do I want my students to become?

LAURA CASSEL

"In the Catholic school's educational project there is no separation between time for learning and time for formation, between acquiring notions and growing in wisdom. The various school subjects do not present only knowledge to be attained, but also values to be acquired and truths to be discovered."

THE CATHOLIC SCHOOL ON THE THRESHOLD OF THE THIRD MILLENNIUM §14

Loving God,
Our Catholic schools are sacred places within Your Kingdom.

Allow them to be
    Places of worship,
    Places of inquiry,
    Places of compassion,
    Places of love,
    Places of evangelization.

Bless our school leaders and teachers to ensure that Your Word remains at the center of our mission.

Empower us with a sense of resolve, loyalty, and commitment to Your Church.

We ask this through Christ, our Lord.
Amen.

                                       CHRISTOPHER BOTT

"The special character of the Catholic school, the underlying reason for it, the reason why Catholic parents should prefer it, is precisely the quality of the religious instruction integrated into the education of the pupils."

CATECHESI TRADENDAE §69

"Hey, did you know that we don't say 'Alleluia' in Lent?" my ten-year-old, Matthew, asks.

After Mass on Pentecost, my son Jacob queries, "Did you know that Ordinary Time begins tomorrow and lasts until Advent?"

Even Joshua, just finishing kindergarten, has chimed in, "Did you know that today is St. Joseph's Day?"

Most Catholic parents would agree that one of the reasons that they have selected Catholic education for their children is for the deep immersion into the faith. An interesting dynamic soon emerges, however, once your children are enrolled in a Catholic school. They bring an unbounded eagerness, enthusiasm, and a sense of wonder to their faith—reigniting the household with their energy. Even though we've sent them to be catechized, they've become the catechists. Sometimes I know the answers to their probing questions, and sometimes I don't, but either way a discussion follows that results in a better understanding on both sides.

They may be fond of quizzing me with Catholic trivia, but when I hear their hearty voices at Mass, observe their heartfelt preparation for First Communion, or listen to their simple prayers for the sick or poor, I know that something deeper is at work. The special character of the Catholic school is making its mark, bringing them ever closer to a life of faith.

JIM FRABUTT

"The future of Catholic school education depends on the entire Catholic community embracing wholeheartedly the concept of stewardship of time, talent, and treasure, and translating stewardship into concrete action."

RENEWING OUR COMMITMENT pp. 10-11

---

1. When were you last aware of a talent of yours at work? Describe how it felt and how it affected others.

2. Do we see our stewardship as gifts of ourselves offered in sacrifice in the Holy Eucharist? How might doing so make such weekly practice more meaningful? ("Pray, that our sacrifice may be acceptable...please accept this offering at your hands, for the praise and glory of your name, for our good and the good of all the Church"). Remember, too, our baptismal call to be a priestly people.

3. When did you last name a talent of another, pointing it out for another to see, in thanks or recognition? Think about a time when someone did that for you. How did that affect you and the other person? Do we do that enough? What holds us back, if not?

SORIN ENGELLAND-SPOHN

"Every Christian, and therefore also every lay person, has been made a sharer in 'the priestly, prophetic, and kingly functions of Christ' and their apostolate 'is a participation in the saving mission of the Church itself....All are commissioned to that apostolate by the Lord Himself.'"

LAY CATHOLICS IN SCHOOLS §6

Almighty Father,
Through our baptism, we share in Your Son's role as
priest, prophet, and king. May we be made sharers in the
priesthood of Jesus Christ by offering lives full of good
works.

May our joys and our sorrows, our successes and our
disappointments, become a living sacrifice of praise
acceptable to You.

Inspired by Your Holy Spirit, may we be prophets of hope as
we preach the truth without fear, and may the testimony of
our lives be an eloquent witness to Jesus in the world.

Enkindle in our hearts a true spirit of kingly service so that
we may always be eager to reach out to those in need. May
we be obedient sons and daughters of Your Church, using
the gifts You have given to us to bring about the Kingdom
of Christ in a world that is thirsting for You.

Through the intercession of Mary, our Mother, we ask that
You grant us all these things, through Jesus Christ, our Lord.
Amen.

SISTER ANNE CATHERINE BURLEIGH, O.P.

"Teaching has an extraordinary moral depth and is one of man's most excellent and creative activities, for the teacher does not write on inanimate material, but on the very spirits of human beings."

THE CATHOLIC SCHOOL ON THE THRESHOLD OF THE THIRD MILLENNIUM §19

---

*E*ducators do not work on an assembly line where consistent, exacting precision produces the same final product. Writing on the spirit of our students often does not come easily. Instead, our work, guided by the Holy Spirit, calls us to be informed about and considerate of all that surrounds each student. It requires teachers to be knowledgeable of their curricula, aware of the limitations of each student, in touch with the environment surrounding that student, and in possession of a plan that will ensure content mastery.

Those who have chosen to teach in Catholic schools, when fully knowledgeable of the mission of their ministry, understand the demands that will be placed upon them. Successful administrators understand that establishing a partnership between teachers and parents is crucial in building a successful school environment.

"You gave me wings" is what the speaker said at the podium. His words came through tears and from the depth of his soul. He spoke to me. He apologized to those gathered for the baccalaureate Mass for all the problems he had caused while a student in the school. He acknowledged that I had been tough when he needed toughness, had remained firm in my expectations of him, and had been compassionate when he needed to be lifted and held. I listened with my heart. How many administrators are privileged to hear words like this spoken aloud? Yes, the days had been long. The problems had been numerous. The conferences had been frequent. But, the expectation remained the same: you have value, you have God-given talents, you can be productive, but you have to rise to the expectations that we have for you.

Am I an assembly line worker? Definitely not! The work of a school administrator is demanding but rewarding beyond measure. While we may not always hear words like these, we have the opportunity to watch students leave our care and move on to the next challenge in their life. Our reward comes from seeing their success and knowing that we had a small part in that accomplishment.

ROSANN WHITING

"Since the educative mission of the Catholic school is so wide, the teacher is in an excellent position to guide the pupil to a deepening of his faith and to enrich and enlighten his human knowledge with the data of the faith."

THE CATHOLIC SCHOOL §40

---

1. What are the indicators in a Catholic school that the school is living out its educative mission?

2. What are the implications for a Catholic school principal that the teacher serves as a guide for pupils in deepening their faith?

3. What are some practical strategies that Catholic school teachers can use in the content areas to enrich and enlighten human knowledge for pupils with the data of faith?

BROTHER WILLIAM DYGERT, C.S.C.

"To use the words of Leo XIII: 'It is necessary not only that religious instruction be given to the young at certain fixed times, but also that every other subject taught, be permeated with Christian piety. If this is wanting, if this sacred atmosphere does not pervade and warm the hearts of masters and scholars alike, little good can be expected from any kind of learning, and considerable harm will often be the consequence.'"

DIVINI ILIUS MAGISTRI §80

Heavenly Father,
Soften my heart to be open to the "sacred atmosphere" of this school. Harden my resolve to draw students closer to You, through every deed.

Open my mind to creatively incorporate the Good News in all my teaching. Close out any doubt that may distract me from my vocation.

Enkindle my spirit to be a light that leads others to You. Quench all thirst for personal gain and glory.

Draw me in closer to You each day. Send me out to do Your will in this world.
Amen.

ANTHONY HOLTER

"Our Church and our nation have been enriched because of the quality of education provided in Catholic schools over the last 300 years. We express our deep and prayerful thanks to the religious, priests, and laity who have formed this ministry. Now we are called to sustain and expand this vitally important ministry of the Church."

IN SUPPORT OF CATHOLIC ELEMENTARY AND SECONDARY SCHOOLS p. 9

---

*O*ften "thank you's" are appropriate at the conclusion of an endeavor. We say "thank you" to the student for a job well done and express gratitude to parents for their support at the end of a season, performance, or field trip. So, we might conclude that it would be better to avoid expressing prayerful thanks to the religious, priests, and laity who have served in our schools for over 300 years because we do not want to suggest that something is completed, or an era ended. However, we need only turn to the Eucharist for a paradigm of gratitude that looks forward to the future and energizes, nourishes, and sustains those who share it.

Eucharist is a term derived from the Greek verb *eucharistein*, "to say thank you." How does one say "thank you" to God? By sharing in the Eucharist offered by His Son, Jesus Christ. This means we express our gratitude through living the Eucharist by being what we are, members of the Body of Christ, literally images of Christ going forth and being Christ for the world. It is in this sense that we most eloquently say "thank you" to those Catholic school educators who preceded us.

Where the Eucharist encourages and nourishes us as Catholic Christians in the world, our gratitude to those who preceded us in ministry to Catholic schools ought to likewise challenge and nurture us as we sustain and expand their ministry for the Church.

MAX ENGEL

"It would be wrong to consider subjects as mere adjuncts to faith or as a useful means of teaching apologetics. They enable the pupil to assimilate skills, knowledge, intellectual methods and moral and social attitudes, all of which help to develop his personality and lead him to take his place as an active member of the community of man. Their aim is not merely the attainment of knowledge but the acquisition of values and the discovery of truth."

THE CATHOLIC SCHOOL §49

Heavenly Father,
Let me be an instrument of grace rather than judgment for families and communities that I may not have the wisdom to fully understand, but have nonetheless been called to serve.

I believe the decisions I make every day make an immeasurable impact on students, families, and the community. Help me stay strong in my convictions, actions, and decisions, while not being crushed by the gravity of my calling.

Support me as I lead students to a more enlightened vision of themselves and You through their coursework. Help them see the connections between their academic pursuits and their ability to serve You.

Lead me to seek out opportunities for my students to engage with the curriculum in ways that allow them to uncover the gifts You have bestowed upon them.

In thanksgiving for my many blessings as Your servant through education,
Amen.

AZURE SMILEY

"The Catholic school acts as the Christian ferment of the world. In it, students learn to overcome individualism and to discover, in the light of faith, that they are called to live responsibly a specific vocation to friendship with Christ and in solidarity with other persons. Basically, the school is called to be a living witness of the love of God among us."

EDUCATING TOGETHER IN CATHOLIC SCHOOLS §46

---

1. Does your school teach students the strength, power, and beauty of community? If so, in what ways are these observable?

2. In what ways are students in your school taught to live as Christian witnesses?

3. How are students in your school called to friendship in Christ?

4. How do you help students in your school discover this friendship?

5. How do you contribute to your school being an example of God's love to the world?

DAN TULLY

> *"Today's Catholic school is more than a means for safeguarding faith and virtue; it is a center in which parents and teachers, guided by the Holy Spirit, collaborate in giving children a complete Catholic education."*

TEACH THEM! §28

In one of my ministries a number of years ago, I was principal in a small Catholic all women's high school. As we approached the first parent-teacher conference, I remember some of the newer teachers viewing this forthcoming event with some trepidation and nervous anticipation. I realized that the teachers were used to a classroom of adolescents but were shy about entering a conversation with other adults!

One of the tremendous advantages we have as Catholic school educators is that parents or guardians have often sacrificed to send their son or daughter to the Catholic school. While it is no guarantee that the parents or guardians will be involved, making such a financial sacrifice gives an incentive that our public school counterparts do not have. While we are also part of a society in which parents often feel they know what is best for their child, the challenge for Catholic educators is to enter any conversation with parents with one thing in mind—the face of the young Catholic student.

One of the values that Catholic educators espouse is that we educate the whole child—we are concerned about the attainment of specific knowledge but we also nurture the young person physically and spiritually. Entering into conversation with the parents brings those values to the home as well as the school. Do we always agree? No, but what a wonderful opportunity for conversation and dialogue, modeling for the student not only Christian values but how to deal with differences, while respecting the individual.

As educators, we are but one leg of the three-legged stool—parents, student, and educator—desiring to prepare young people for the future, grounded in the Catholic faith.

SISTER MARY JANE HERB, I.H.M.

"If a school is excellent as an academic institution, but does not witness to authentic values, then both good pedagogy and a concern for pastoral care make it obvious that renewal is called for—not only in the content and methodology of religious instruction, but in the overall school planning which governs the whole process of formation of the students."

THE RELIGIOUS DIMENSION OF EDUCATION IN A CATHOLIC SCHOOL §19

1. How does my school integrate the faith into all it does?

2. What visible signs are there in my school that clearly demonstrate that faith is at the heart of all we do?

3. Does the school calendar clearly reflect the importance of my school's Catholic identity?

4. What opportunities do the students at my school have to share their faith with one another?

PATRICK FENNESSY

"For it is the lay teachers, and indeed all lay persons, believers or not, who will substantially determine whether or not a school realizes its aims and accomplishes its objectives. In the Second Vatican Council, and specifically in the Declaration on Christian Education, the Church recognized the role and the responsibility that this situation confers on all those lay Catholics who work in any type of elementary and secondary schools, whether as teachers, directors, administrators, or auxiliary staff."

LAY CATHOLICS IN SCHOOLS §1

Heavenly Father,
By our Baptism, You have called each of us to share in the teaching and sanctifying mission of Jesus.

As the people of God, and guided by the Holy Spirit, we are called to be the presence of Christ in word and deed to all those we encounter. As ministers called to the apostolate of Catholic education, we ask You to bless all those who serve in Catholic schools.

We pray in gratitude for all those who work behind the scenes—the office workers, the facilities and maintenance personnel, and all other staff members—without whose daily commitment our schools would not be able to remain open.

We pray in thanksgiving for the important role that teachers play in advancing a commitment to the truth that serves the human person.

Finally, we gratefully pray for school leaders and pastors, whose vision ensures that all who desire the gift of Catholic education may receive its fruitful blessings.

We ask all these things through Christ, our Lord.
Amen.

PETER CORRIGAN

"Creating readiness for growth in community through worship and through the events of everyday life is an integral part of the task of Catholic education, which also seeks to build community within its own programs and institutions."

TO TEACH AS JESUS DID §25

---

*C*atholic identity is an added element to everyday academics that distinguishes a Catholic institution from private or public schools. It is most beautiful to recognize the inevitable moments when worship and everyday events overlap at school. Whether it is a weekly Mass, a morning prayer service, or a faith talk, the atmosphere in such school gatherings encompasses a warm sense of community centered in worship. Students attend and participate in these events with the same peers with whom they study. Just as students of any school may spend time together in the afternoons and may allocate some of that time to finishing homework or discussing their class work, students in Catholic schools share something beyond a common curriculum: they share worship and centeredness in the value of service to God and one another. A Catholic education is an endless invitation to merge worship and work, study and social settings. Students juggle so much as they sort through these facets of their lives, but the integrative community embodied by Catholic education also fosters each student's personal development.

MELISSA REGAN

"Our call now is to all who see with undimmed sight this same apostolic responsibility as their own and will join in carrying out this commitment in the years ahead: the commitment of handing on the faith to the next generation, not merely preserved, but more glorious, more efficacious, more valued by those who in their turn will take up the charge to 'go and teach.'"

TEACH THEM! §46

---

1. What will American Catholic elementary and secondary education look like in 2020?

2. What can you do within the confines of your role as a member of the Catholic school community to ensure that our schools thrive for future generations?

3. What must we hold as sacred as we evolve into the Catholic schools of the twenty-first century?

4. How can Catholic communities maintain focus, a positive outlook, and a collaborative approach as we address these challenging topics?

CHRISTOPHER BOTT

"The Catholic school forms part of the saving mission of the Church, especially for education in the faith."

THE CATHOLIC SCHOOL §9

Heavenly Father,
Help our school bring students closer to You through education about their faith.

Give our teachers the ability to educate the mind, body and spirit of each child, that each student feels fulfilled.

Grant our school staff and faculty the grace to be patient yet persistent in our mission.

Allow our work to build in each child a foundation for our faith that they may come to understand, embrace, and defend it.

Use our school as Your workshop on earth, creating followers who will continue in Your saving mission.
Amen.

ANNE CHRISTINE BARBERA

"Education itself must be seen as the acquisition, growth and possession of freedom. It is a matter of educating each student to free him/herself from the conditionings that prevent him/her from fully living as a person, to form him/herself into a strong and responsible personality, capable of making free and consistent choices."

CONSECRATED PERSONS AND THEIR MISSION IN SCHOOLS §52

A religious sister takes three vows: poverty, chastity, and obedience. For some, these vows may seem restrictive—the loss of material goods, a husband and family, and independence. In reality, they provide freedom from the burden of possessions, to dedicate one's life to the service of God, and to be a part of something bigger than oneself. Our students face the same temptations: consumerism, sexism, and individualism. They surround our students in the media, on the Internet, and in our schools.

Children are exposed at a very early age to the idea that owning things makes them happy. Can we give them alternative experiences that help them see that real happiness comes from reaching out to help others?

Many young people believe that physical perfection will make them happy. Can we help them see themselves as God does, freeing them from the need to compare themselves to celebrities and allowing them to concentrate on being comfortable in their own skins?

So many of our students are seduced by individualism. If they cannot do or learn something on their own, they become frustrated and quit. Group projects so often become divide and conquer instead of a collaborative effort. Can we teach them how to work cooperatively? Do we model cooperation?

Just as a sister's vows provide her freedom, administrators and teachers at a Catholic school can model, make students aware, facilitate, and reward countercultural behavior in our students, allowing them the freedom to become what God intends them to be.

SISTER BARBARA KANE, O.P.

132

"Only one who has this conviction and accepts Christ's message, who has a love for and understands today's young people, who appreciates what people's real problems and difficulties are, will be led to contribute with courage and even audacity to the progress of this apostolate in building up a Catholic school, which puts its theory into practice, which renews itself according to its ideals and to present needs."

THE CATHOLIC SCHOOL §83

---

1. Think about the students whose lives you touch. Is there one student in particular that you find difficult to love? Think about ways that you can begin to see God's presence in that student.

2. Think about your interactions with your co-workers at school, particularly in the faculty room. Are there ways that you can be an example to them in the way you discuss your students?

3. In what ways do you let your students know that you love them all and truly believe that they are created in God's image and likeness?

PAMELA LYONS

"The Catholic school participates in this mission like a true ecclesial subject, with its educational service that is enlivened by the truth of the Gospel. In fact, faithful to its vocation, it appears 'as a place of integral education of the human person through a clear educational project of which Christ is the foundation,' directed at creating a synthesis between faith, culture and life."

EDUCATING TOGETHER IN CATHOLIC SCHOOLS §3

Creator God, source of all that is good,
You set the rhythm of the universe, gracefully orchestrating the stars in the heavens. Out of nothingness You created and worlds came to be.

With hearts full of gratitude and minds filled with wonder, we contemplate the majesty of it all. We see the stars highlighting the heavens, the moon shining above, the sun rising and setting on all Your hand has created.

Grant us awe in Your presence as we meditate on Your glory. Give us peace in our hearts as we gaze on Your handiwork. Fill us with humility as we pray to find our place and our work in this universe.

May all of creation sing in one voice so that we may recognize the fullness of joy in that Kingdom where Jesus is Lord forever and ever.
Amen.

FATHER RONALD NUZZI

"The State and the Church have the obligation to give families all possible aid to enable them to perform their educational role properly. Therefore both the Church and the State must create and foster the institutions and activities that families justly demand, and the aid must be in proportion to the families' needs. However, those in society who are in charge of schools must never forget that the parents have been appointed by God Himself as the first and principal educators of their children and that their right is completely inalienable."

FAMILIARIS CONSORTIO §40

There are occasions in my life as a parent where I am reminded of the important and sacred role my wife and I share as principal educators of our children. One such moment occurred recently when we began visiting schools and considering programs for our oldest daughter, who is of preschool age.

The choice for us was a simple one; our daughter would attend a school where the faith we practice at home permeated the environment, instruction, and relationships where she would begin her formal education. This principle had always been clear to me as an educator—something I often discussed with students and colleagues—but really came to life when it was time for us to choose a school for our daughter, our first student.

For us, and for our daughter, Catholic schools are not simply "a" choice among many options, but "the" choice for a school that honors and builds on the primary education in the faith that our daughter receives at home.

ANTHONY HOLTER

"With good reason therefore did St. John Chrysostom say, 'What greater work is there than training the mind and forming the habits of the young?'"

DIVINI ILIUS MAGISTRI §8

---

1. As an administrator, how can I best serve the students in my care? Are there special skills that I lack that would assist me in working well with each student?

2. As an administrator, how can I remind my faculty that their work transcends the curriculum that they teach? How can I ensure that each day the faculty recognizes the importance of their work? How can I choose the words and actions to remind others that molding a child in the image of God is a privilege few people are given?

3. As an administrator, how can I be present for the parents and assist them in the development of their child? This work can be time consuming and painfully difficult. How can I ensure that I will listen with my heart and my ears?

ROSANN WHITING

"Education is one of the most important ways by which the Church fulfills its commitment to the dignity of the person and the building of community."

TO TEACH AS JESUS DID §13

Dear Lord,
Help me see the possibilities in each child, no matter how deeply they may be hidden.

Encourage me to recognize the failures of my students and myself as an opportunity to grow together.

Support me as I embrace reconciliation and teach my students to do the same.

Help me see past current trends and noise, to stay faithful to my mission and beliefs.

Let me see times of struggle in my profession as an opportunity to stay true to what I believe and show my devotion to You through my actions and decisions.

Guide me as I walk my talk and illuminate the path for others to the Good News of the Lord.

Help me feel the presence of the Holy Spirit as I foster the development of our future community leaders to grow in Your love.

In thanksgiving for the responsibility bestowed upon me through my calling to serve You,
Amen.

AZURE SMILEY

"Many of the students will attend a Catholic school—often the same school—from the time they are very young children until they are nearly adults. It is only natural that they should come to think of the school as an extension of their own homes, and therefore a 'school-home' ought to have some of the amenities which can create a pleasant and family atmosphere."

THE RELIGIOUS DIMENSION OF EDUCATION IN A CATHOLIC SCHOOL §27

If someone asked you to define what a school is, what answer would you give them? The dictionary tells us that schools are institutions where instruction is given to children under college age. What about a Catholic school? Would anything change in your definition?

Think about how much time you personally spend at school, whether it be grading papers or joking around with students. It might be hard to believe how much time and dedication you put in when you actually stop to think about it. Now think about how much time your students spend at school.

It should be clear that a Catholic school is much more than some institution where instruction is given. Instead, it is a place where the full person is developed and appreciated. It is truly a second home for many and in some instances, the only home for others.

How do you facilitate a family environment in your role as a Catholic school leader? Too often, we get caught up in the technical side of education involving grades and test scores without considering the human element of education.

As Christians and Catholics, we are all called to encourage and promote a community of faith, hope, and love in all that we do. You, as a Catholic school leader, have an even greater calling to this work, by molding young men and women to be future leaders of the world.

The ideals of community and family should not be confined to someone's personal home; instead, they should be even more deeply promoted within the walls of the classroom. Combining the opportunity for one to grow in knowledge and spirit is a unique characteristic of Catholic schools, and it is successfully done by creating an environment where students and parents feel like they are at their second home—one of welcome and love.

KEVIN KIMBERLY

"So indeed the Catholic school, while it is open, as it must be, to the situation of the contemporary world, leads its students to promote efficaciously the good of the earthly city and also prepares them for service in the spread of the Kingdom of God, so that by leading an exemplary apostolic life they become, as it were, a saving leaven in the human community."

GRAVISSIMUM EDUCATIONIS §8

Dear God,
We live in a conflicted modern world.

Help us to be Your representatives in this world so that through education we can guide minds to serve Your Kingdom both here on earth and eternally.

Help us to spread Your love with our actions, and guide our hearts so that we can more fully learn and discern Your work.

We ask this through Your Son, our most important teacher. Amen.

RACHEL ROSEBERRY

"As we, the Catholic bishops of the United States, and the entire Catholic community continue our journey through the twenty-first century, it remains our duty to model the Person of Jesus Christ, to teach the Gospel, and to evangelize our culture. We are convinced that Catholic elementary and secondary schools play a critical role in this endeavor."

RENEWING OUR COMMITMENT p. 14

1. How can my school help students understand the importance of modeling their lives after Jesus Christ?

2. By providing daily suggestions and incorporating the mission of Jesus in the classroom, how are we as a school improving the lives of all of God's children?

3. Through prayer and service, we as a school work toward becoming closer to God, but how can we evangelize our culture in a more permanent way?

4. How can we encourage our students to continue this work in their daily lives in order to create lasting change?

ANNE CHRISTINE BARBERA

"The Catholic Church has consistently held that one of its primary functions is the education of young people. In the United States, the Church can proudly point to a positive and productive record of serving the educational needs of our nation's young people almost from the nation's first days."

PRINCIPLES FOR EDUCATIONAL REFORM IN THE UNITED STATES p. 2

Lord,
Your Catholic schools bring us closer to You. Since our nation's earliest days, Catholic teachers have been here, sharing Your Word.

Bless our schools that are struggling, the ones that need more students, and more financial support. Fill our Catholic schools with the most faithful and experienced leaders to help them flourish.

Help us continue to point our children in positive and pro-ductive directions. Our Catholic schools can transform the nation's children with Your help.

Be present in our schools and in us so that we may keep them fully alive. In Your name we pray.
Amen.

CHRISTIE HJERPE

"Therefore, 'the laity are called in a special way to make the Church present and operative in those places and circumstances where only through them can she become the salt of the earth.' In order to achieve this presence of the whole Church, and of the Saviour whom she proclaims, lay people must be ready to proclaim the message through their words, and witness to it in what they do."

LAY CATHOLICS IN SCHOOLS §9

Strong academics. Focus on the individual. Better than average test scores. Teaching to the entire person. Preparation for higher education. Life skills. Schools have so many different goals to achieve. If you have ever listened to educators attempt to bring a new family to their school, they most likely used catch phrases like these to grab the family's attention.

As Catholic educators though, we are called to do so much more. We are called to make Christ ever present. We are called to make Christ the center of what we do. Christ should not simply be in our mission statements. He should be the first thing we think to share in our schools.

The landscape of Catholic schools has changed drastically over the last seventy-five years. There was once a time when lay people had very little presence in Catholic schools. The charge of the religious education of our young people was placed at the feet of those that had taken religious vows. Each day it becomes rarer to find those that have consecrated their lives to God involved in the day-to-day operation of our schools. The mantle of Catholic education has been passed to the lay people who organize, run, and plan for the future of our schools, taking on this sacred charge of religious education for our young people.

As lay ministers, how are we doing? Do we have Christ everpresent in our schools? Do our students see the face of Christ in the adults that surround them as they struggle through the challenges of growing up?

I once had a student that wrote me a letter. She had been struggling with bullies on the playground. As I read her letter, my heart went out to this young person who was trying to follow in Christ's way. As she wrapped up her note, she explained to me why she had chosen to ask me for help. She said, "Your voice is like an angel. I knew you could help."

In a world filled with so much evil and sadness, our children still look for signs of the divine around them. It is our duty to be that for them. Christ must be present through us for our young people. They are watching; are you witnessing?

HEATHER LINDSAY

"A teacher who is full of Christian wisdom, well prepared in his own subject, does more than convey the sense of what he is teaching to his pupils. Over and above what he says, he guides his pupils beyond his mere words to the heart of total Truth."

THE CATHOLIC SCHOOL §41

1. How does a Catholic school teacher infuse the pursuit of truth throughout his or her lessons?

2. How would a school measure whether students have reached "the heart of total Truth"?

3. Can Catholic school administrators identify if a teacher is "full of Christian wisdom"?

LORI MOREAU

"New horizons will be opened to students through the responses that Christian revelation brings to questions about the ultimate meaning of the human person, of human life, of history, and of the world. These must be offered to the students as responses which flow out of the profound faith of the educator, but at the same time with the greatest sensitive respect for the conscience of each student."

LAY CATHOLICS IN SCHOOLS §28

Dear Lord,
Help me see You in every child I encounter today.

Help me let go of the assumptions I may have about my students so I can more clearly see how I might help them become the people You wish them to be.

Help me set a good example for my co-workers in the way I talk about my students. Let me be a gentle reminder that each student is created in Your image and likeness.

Help me show my students that I love them all regardless of their performance in school, family situation or behavior.

Show me ways that I can create an atmosphere in my classroom where all students know that they are God's beloveds.
Amen.

PAMELA LYONS

"Since it is motivated by the Christian ideal, the Catholic school is particularly sensitive to the call from every part of the world for a more just society, and it tries to make its own contribution towards it. It does not stop at the courageous teaching of the demands of justice even in the face of local opposition, but tries to put these demands into practice in its own community in the daily life of the school."

THE CATHOLIC SCHOOL §58

The mission of our school is to provide students with "an education that is founded on a love of God and service to others, characterized by Catholic values and academic excellence." Service is at the heart of this mission, and with Christ as the model, our perspective on service begins with the Gospel teachings.

Our students learn from a very young age how to treat one another with consideration, how to share, and what it means to follow the "golden rule." From there we help the students take responsibility in service initiatives, and by the time they are in the eighth grade, they are ready to lead service projects.

They have learned that we must be good stewards of the earth, and as a result began a recycling, composting, and an eco-friendly landscaping project. They have also learned that we do not live in isolation, and that our actions have global impact. With this understanding, our student council orchestrated a Pennies for Peace drive, in which they raised thousands of dollars to benefit schools in Afghanistan by reaching out to our school and parish community, as well as the local neighborhood.

Our students have also gone to the grounds of the Capitol Building to voice support for the Opportunity Scholarship Fund, which enabled some of their classmates to attend our school. Each of these initiatives, as well as the many others undertaken, is an extension of the academic curriculum, so the students undoubtedly grow to understand the importance of knowledge and how they should use it to benefit the world, both globally and locally.

JENNIFER KETCHUM

"With kindness and understanding, [teachers] will accept the students as they are, helping them to see that doubt and indifference are common phenomena, and that the reasons for this are readily understandable. But they will invite students in a friendly manner to seek and discover together the message of the Gospel, the source of joy and peace."

THE RELIGIOUS DIMENSION OF EDUCATION IN A CATHOLIC SCHOOL §71

Heavenly Father,
Let all that we do as educators in the faith be addressed to the hearts of those we serve.

Grant us a disposition that is considerate of our students, appreciative of their talents and needs, and generous in mercy toward them.

May our classrooms be distinguished by warmth and permeated by the Gospel spirit of freedom and love.

Through the inspiration of Your Holy Spirit, may we be a medium of Your grace to those we teach.

Grant us the grace of good example that we may model by who we are and how we live, as well as by what we say, the true peace and joy that flows from a relationship with Jesus Christ.
Amen.

BROTHER WILLIAM DYGERT, C.S.C.

"The Catholic school is not simply an institution which offers academic instruction of high quality, but, even more important, is an effective vehicle of total Christian formation. The tendency to emphasize one aspect at the expense of the other has given way to recognition that both are necessary and possible, and indeed are being accomplished in Catholic schools."

TEACH THEM! §21

---

1. How can you as a leader ensure that the balance between academic instruction and Christian formation is achieved?

2. What checks are in place to maintain the Catholic identity of your school?

3. How do you facilitate excellent academics? What can you do today to call students to their best academic performance and a strong faith life?

MICHELLE RYAN

"It is, therefore, very desirable that every lay Catholic educator become fully aware of the importance, the richness, and the responsibility of this vocation. They should fully respond to all of its demands, secure in the knowledge that their response is vital for the construction and ongoing renewal of the earthly city, and for the evangelization of the world."

LAY CATHOLICS IN SCHOOLS §37

A student of mine once told me, "Miss H, you are a tank." A tank!? I was confused. In my head I pictured a large military tank, or a tank meaning someone who could consume a lot of alcohol. I didn't ask him to clarify. Instead, I got in my own head. Did I offend him? Do I look like a tank? Am I that ugly?

These thoughts consumed my brain. Why did he call me a tank? After sitting on it for a few hours I confronted him and asked him to clarify.

"Joe," I said as I approached him after lunch, "what did you mean when you called me a tank?" Joe laughed and said very confidently: "Miss H, you are a tank. I love your class, and your faith is so strong, and so indestructible...it's like...it's like a tank. A tank is cool."

It was in that very moment that I felt God calling me to teach in Catholic schools. Joe, a high school junior, gave me one of the best compliments I have ever received. I am a tank. My faith is indestructible.

So is my passion for Catholic schools. As a result, I want to share it, and that is why I teach. My vocation is full of richness and responsibility. I hope that my confidence, strength, and compassion radiate onto my students. When I receive compliments like the one Joe gave me—representing creative, inspirational, different ways of thinking—I know I am making a difference. Silly words like "tank" are God's way of telling me not to go anywhere. A tank is pretty stationary—and I'm not leaving these kids.

CHRISTIE HJERPE

"All those involved in a Catholic school—parents, pastors, teachers, administrators, and students—must earnestly desire to make it a community of faith which is indeed 'living, conscious and active.'"

TO TEACH AS JESUS DID §106

Loving God,
You have called us to serve You through our involvement in Catholic schools.

> Energize our teachers to model Your love for their students, so through them they see Christ;

> Enliven our pastors to provide vibrant leadership to all they serve;

> Instill Your example of compassionate leadership in our administrators so they may be Christ for others;

> Open the minds and hearts of our students so that they are open to the wonders of Your creation;

> Strengthen our parents to raise their children to be active participants in Your Church.

Watch over us all, so we may continue to strengthen and sustain Catholic schools.
Amen.

PATRICK FENNESSY

"In these schools the liberty of parents is respected; and, what is most needed, especially in the prevailing license of opinion and of action, it is by these schools that good citizens are brought up for the State; for there is no better citizen than the man who has believed and practiced the Christian faith from his childhood."

SPECTATA FIDES §4

---

1. How does our school promote good citizenship through service and responsibility to be active in the community?

2. Do we provide concrete examples and suggestions to help students understand what it means to be a good citizen, not only to their local community, but to the world?

3. Have we prepared our students to be patriotic but also to defend their faith when the interests of the nation and the Church conflict?

SORIN ENGELLAND-SPOHN

"The integration of religious truth and values with the rest of life, which is possible in these schools, distinguishes them from others. Here the Catholic for whom religious commitment is a matter of central importance finds an appreciation of religion which parallels his or her own."

TEACH THEM! §9

---

*A*s a young child, I did not understand the importance of my education in a Catholic elementary school. Although I spent six years at my parish school, I did not appreciate my experiences until I attended public school and realized the differences. Although the teachers were smart and kind in both schools, the teachers in the Catholic school invested much more time and effort into my development as an individual.

Reflecting upon my experiences, I realize that the reason for this attention is the mission of Catholic schools, that of developing the mind and spirit of every one of God's children. This mission differentiates Catholic schools from all other schools because of the emphasis on holistic development.

Teachers were concerned with imparting knowledge but also with conveying the importance of including Christian principles in every aspect of life. They also reinforced morals and values that my parents emphasized in my home, giving me a better basis for my beliefs.

In addition to providing reinforcement for my values, attending a Catholic school gave me the opportunity to participate in service-learning activities. These experiences helped me to realize the importance of combining my religious education with my practical knowledge gained in school.

The many lessons I learned in Catholic schools about caring for the entire individual and incorporating God into daily life have led me to appreciate my Catholic upbringing.

ANNE CHRISTINE BARBERA

"It is, in fact, through the school that [the Church] participates in the dialogue of culture with her own positive contribution to the cause of the total formation of man [and woman]. The absence of the Catholic school would be a great loss for civilization and for the natural destiny of man [and woman]."

THE CATHOLIC SCHOOL §15

Generous and Faithful God,
You choose to reveal Yourself in many ways and powerfully through the love of teachers for their students.

Through our efforts, we strive to form students into young women and men who
    respect and care for their bodies,
    seek truth through study,
    see others as their brothers and sisters,
    recognize the value and beauty of nature,
    develop the talents You bestowed in them,
    and welcome the outsider into their midst.

Above all, loving God, we strive to imitate Your Son
Jesus, so that our students will see how to be loving and compassionate and will model that behavior to others.

Your fidelity gives us hope that our efforts will not be in vain and that our students will become all that You intend them to be.
Amen.

SISTER BARBARA KANE, O.P.

"The success of the Church's educational mission will also be judged by how well it helps the Catholic community to see the dignity of human life with the vision of Jesus and involve itself in the search for solutions to the pressing problems of society."

TO TEACH AS JESUS DID §10

---

1. Identify three concrete ways that your faculty and students uphold the dignity of human life with the vision of Jesus.

2. This excerpt challenges Catholic schools to be places where faith leads to action. In what ways does your school engage with the pressing problems of society?

3. What outreach, service, or ministry opportunities does your school offer as "solutions" to the pressing problems of society?

JIM FRABUTT

"Conduct is always much more important than speech; this fact becomes especially important in the formation period of students. The more completely an educator can give concrete witness to the model of the ideal person that is being presented to the students, the more this ideal will be believed and imitated."

LAY CATHOLICS IN SCHOOLS §32

Our actions speak so loudly that our words cannot be heard. So it is in the life of an educator. We are called to be examples to the young people we serve and we are always in their line of vision. Young people have an ardent desire for authentic role models. They seek someone who will prove, by the integrity of his or her life, that living the Christian life is possible and that it brings peace and joy.

On a daily basis, how do we model Christian life? Does our life radiate the happiness of knowing that we are loved and cherished by our God? Do we have integrity? Is the life we teach in the classroom the life that we lead outside of school? We cannot only partially answer the call to holiness. We have to give our full consent and put all of our energy and desire into striving for holiness of life. We will be credible witnesses of the Gospel only if we truly seek to do God's will in each moment and allow Him to use us as His instruments in the work of spreading the Gospel through Catholic education. The greatness of the task can be overwhelming. Saint Paul, through his example, gives us hope when we fall short of the goal.

Saint Paul laments in the Letter to the Romans that he often chose the evil he did not intend and failed to do the good he did intend (Romans 7:15-25). His struggle resonates with each of us as we examine our thoughts, words, and actions at the end of each day. We strive daily to grow in virtue, only to see that there is still more work to do in order to become the person God desires us to be. How important to remember that Saint Paul concluded his statements about this struggle by giving everything over to the Lord Jesus. "Thanks be to God through Jesus Christ our Lord" (Romans 7:25). It is the Lord who accomplishes any good that may come of our efforts.

SISTER JOHN PAUL MYERS, O.P.

"Because its aim is to make man more man, education can be carried out authentically only in a relational and community context."

EDUCATING TOGETHER IN CATHOLIC SCHOOLS §12

Heavenly Father,
You have blessed us with remarkable religious and lay teachers. Their contributions to our schools have been exceptional.

Allow them to
    Live the Gospel;
    Love their students;
    Inspire greatness;
    Encourage academic curiosity;
    And cultivate sound values.

We ask this through Jesus Christ, our Lord.
Amen.

CHRISTOPHER BOTT

"For the Catholic educator, religious formation does not come to an end with the completion of basic education; it must be a part of and a complement to one's professional formation, and so be proportionate to adult faith, human culture, and the specific lay vocation."

LAY CATHOLICS IN SCHOOLS §65

---

1. How can we, as educators, ensure that we grow in faith every day, that we may model this for our students?

2. Do I make time in my daily schedule to include prayer, even when it's difficult to get everything ready for classes?

3. Does my faith formation revolve around school, Sunday Mass and holidays? How can I include more spontaneous prayer in order to grow closer to God?

ANNE CHRISTINE BARBERA

"The nobility of the task to which teachers are called demands that, in imitation of Christ, the only Teacher, they reveal the Christian message not only by word but also by every gesture of their behavior. This is what makes the difference between a school whose education is permeated by the Christian spirit and one in which religion is only regarded as an academic subject like any other."

THE CATHOLIC SCHOOL §43

The demands on a Catholic school administrator or teacher are great. We are called upon to provide sound instruction, acknowledging the best in pedagogy. We are asked to have masterful command of our content area or domain. We are also asked to occasionally be mentor, coach, advisor, counselor, social worker, and even school nurse. But inside and outside of the classroom, the job of a Catholic school administrator or teacher never ends. We are expected to model Christ's message in our every thought, word, and deed.

It is not uncommon for me to be going about my business, at the store, at a restaurant, or on the street, and be stopped by a student, alumnus, or parent who knows me from our school. But rather than ignore the overture or conversation, I tend to welcome it. It is important for our community to know that we are real people living real lives.

And while we are not perfect people, we are perfect examples of God's people. We face risks and responsibilities. We have friends and families. We do service and share. We worship and pray. We ask our students to be persons of God and we do our best to live our lives similarly.

It is an additional burden to be on our best behavior, knowing that we might encounter someone who knows or recognizes us as a Catholic school teacher or administrator, but it brings me pride to know that I am doing my best to be an example for others. The call is immense and the expectations considerable, but the reward is greater.

DAN TULLY

"Among all educational instruments the school has a special importance. It is designed not only to develop with special care the intellectual faculties but also to form the ability to judge rightly, to hand on the cultural legacy of previous generations, to foster a sense of values, to prepare for professional life."
GRAVISSIMUM EDUCATIONIS §5

Jesus,
You were a teacher of extraordinary measure.

Our school is filled with teachers who want to follow Your footsteps. Guide us in developing students' decision-making skills. Let us not be frustrated by students' bad decisions. Help us see through their eyes, their backgrounds, and their cultures, so we can connect on a deeper level and foster their values.

Each child is a blessing; encourage us to identify and strengthen the gifts and talents of each child. Teach us to be an educational instrument to success.

We pray that our school will continue to support, love, and push our children to achieve their dreams. Bless this day and all days that our community may live in Your light. Amen.

CHRISTIE HJERPE

"One of the fundamental requirements for an educator in a Catholic school is his or her possession of a solid professional formation."

EDUCATING TOGETHER IN CATHOLIC SCHOOLS §21

1. How can we ensure strong preparation for education, beyond obtaining degrees and certifications? How might our spirituality and faith fortify professionalism, perhaps on a daily basis?

2. What role can community play in providing and building confidence for educational readiness?

3. From whom can we seek support in the struggles of our roles in Catholic schools? With whom can we form solidarity in the mission to do our part in fulfilling the goals of Catholic education?

MELISSA REGAN

"And finally, every educator is in need of a permanent and growing charity, in order to love each of the students as an individual created in the image and likeness of God, raised to the status of a child of God by the redemption of Jesus Christ."

LAY CATHOLICS IN SCHOOLS §72

My first year of teaching took place in a second grade classroom at a Catholic school in Oakland, California. My class consisted of sixteen wonderful seven-year-olds, and Sam.

Sam was my biggest challenge. He was always angry and I would walk on eggshells waiting for the small thing that would set him off into a rage. When I looked into the eyes of my other sixteen students they were always ready to please and willing to accept anything I set before them. They were easy to love. Sam, however, was not. I hated feeling that way. I wanted to love Sam as I loved the other students but I found it hard to see the child of God beneath the disrespectful exterior. That is until the Christmas program.

My parents came to school on the evening of the Christmas program to meet my class. The minute my father entered the room, Sam was attached to his side. He was a different child with my father. He was respectful, happy, and eagerly did anything my father asked. I saw a different Sam that evening. It made me realize that Sam's behavior had nothing to do with me. He was struggling with issues that I could never even imagine. Sam was a child of God who needed me more than any of the other students in the classroom.

While Sam continued to challenge me for the rest of the school year, I tried my best to always see the lovely child that I saw the night of the Christmas program. Sam taught me more about being a teacher than any other student I have ever taught. He showed me that God comes in all forms and sometimes we just have to look really hard to see Him.

PAMELA LYONS

"The Catholic school finds its true justification in the mission of the Church; it is based on an educational philosophy in which faith, culture, and life are brought into harmony."

THE RELIGIOUS DIMENSION OF EDUCATION IN A CATHOLIC SCHOOL §34

In order for the mission of the school to be met, a school leader must spend much time keeping the school solvent and running smoothly.

1. How do you balance administrative details with the leadership needed to maintain focus on the true mission of the school?

2. What kind of example did Jesus set as a leader? As a manager?

3. How does prayer life and faith affect your ability to delegate and lead without getting bogged down in administrative details?

MICHELLE RYAN

*"A Catholic school's task is to form Christian men, and, by its
teaching and witness, show non-Christians something of the
mystery of Christ Who surpasses all human understanding."*

THE CATHOLIC SCHOOL §47

Loving God,
One of the clearest messages You send to us is to spread
the great news of Your salvation. We do this because of
faith, not because of sight.

In answering Your call, You have led us to our current work
in Catholic schools to mold and shape the minds of young
men and women. As we watch them grow in faith, may we
continue to be a bold witness to Your love and redeeming
grace. May we provide an education of the whole person—
mind, heart, body, and soul—so that our students may
know how great it is to live as a disciple of Christ.

Give us compassion to act as a friend to all, believer or
non-believer. May the example we set for our students
show all who doubt the deep inspiration You bring to all
who believe. Help us to be inspired by all that has come to
us because of You and all that You have promised.

May You always provide us the strength to be open to Your
call to truly serve and love one another. As we continue to
educate Your children, may we continually educate ourselves in order that we may serve You above all.
Amen.

KEVIN KIMBERLY

"As we continue to address the many and varied needs of our nation's new immigrant population, the Church and its schools are often among the few institutions providing immigrants and newcomers with a sense of welcome, dignity, community, and connection with their spiritual roots."

RENEWING OUR COMMITMENT p. 4

J feel discouraged and depressed as I fill in the dollar amounts on the new applicant's financial aid letter. They have qualified for the maximum award, but I am sure it will not be enough. The Church has welcomed them with open arms, but our schools have come up short. In the eighteen months that they have lived in the United States they have faced great challenges. Terrific efforts were necessary to learn English, secure employment, find a home, and assimilate into this foreign world.

Our diocese, much like many dioceses across the nation, has engaged in tremendous efforts to cultivate relationships with recent immigrants. This family has become active members of their parish and loyal members of the worldwide Catholic Church. Why should Catholic education be out of their reach?

Finance, budgeting, and financial aid are all very complicated issues that most school community members do not engage in. It is a cold and hard world where numbers become as inflexible as the problems they create.

I stare at the financial aid letter on my desk and decide to make phone calls to friends of the school who possess financial resources. I quickly pray that this family finds a way to finance their desire for Catholic education, drop the letter into an envelope, and place the envelope into the outgoing mail.

CHRISTOPHER BOTT

"Every school, and every educator in the school, ought to be striving 'to form strong and responsible individuals, who are capable of making free and correct choices,' thus preparing young people 'to open themselves more and more to reality, and to form in themselves a clear idea of the meaning of life.'"

LAY CATHOLICS IN SCHOOLS §17

---

1. How does our faculty and staff work together and support one another in accomplishing the goals of the school?

2. In what ways are the faculty and staff a community of faith, supporting one another in the deepening of the Christian witness that all are called to provide? Does working in the school help me to become more Christ-like?

3. Does our school reward, extol, and encourage honorable behavior regularly?

4. Is there a Code of Ethics for the faculty and staff?

FATHER RONALD NUZZI

"Catholic education is an expression of the mission entrusted by Jesus to the Church He founded. Through education the Church seeks to prepare its members to proclaim the Good News and to translate this proclamation into action."

TO TEACH AS JESUS DID §7

Good and Gracious God,
We are blessed to share in the teaching mission of Your Son, Jesus Christ. Let us be true to the Gospel values—the values that Jesus taught, lived and died for many years ago.

Let us not only teach these values but let them come alive through our lives so that the students entrusted to our care witness on a daily basis the Good News in action.

No matter what subject we are teaching, let us realize that the Catholic identity of our school must be integrated in all that we do.

More importantly, let us recognize the unique gifts each student brings to our classroom and help us touch the lives of our students so that they will grow into the persons You called them to be.

We ask this prayer, as we ask all things, in the name of the Master Teacher, Jesus Christ.
Amen.

SISTER MARY JANE HERB, I.H.M.

"In today's secularized world, students will see many lay people who call themselves Catholics, but who never take part in liturgy or sacraments. It is very important that they also have the example of lay adults who take such things seriously, who find in them a source and nourishment for Christian living."

LAY CATHOLICS IN SCHOOLS §40

As an elementary student at Our Lady of Mt. Carmel School, I would always peek back over my shoulder during a school Mass and catch a quick glimpse at Aunt Jenny. She didn't drive, but my uncle brought her to daily Mass each morning, or she walked there when the weather was nice. Always arriving early, sometimes as our class walked in, she would give me a wave. I always felt a little special and some comfort knowing that familiar face in the back pew. Never was she absent from a key milestone—First Communion, eighth grade graduation, or Confirmation.

Back at the school, another relative, Aunt Lucille, served as the school librarian. In the early grades, I would see her on our weekly trips to the library, listening to her at story time and getting her advice on which books to pick out. Even as a child, I knew about her huge commitment to the parish—making cavatelli for the parish festival, fundraising for the school, and supporting school plays. Whenever I was a server at Mass, I knew that she was behind the altar, joining her voice to the others in the church choir.

These two women—Italian-Americans with deep ties to their faith—in quiet yet always visible ways demonstrated their love for the liturgy, the sacraments, the Church. Even to a child's eyes, their simple, continuous witness was obvious. Each of us, in our professional roles as teachers and school leaders and in our personal roles as parents, godparents, aunts, and uncles must be mindful of the power and grace to teach by example. It's clear that young eyes are quietly watching, ears carefully listening—sometimes internalizing deep truths about their faith.

JIM FRABUTT

"The Catholic school sets out to be a school for the human person and of human persons. 'The person of each individual human being, in his or her material and spiritual needs, is at the heart of Christ's teaching: this is why the promotion of the human person is the goal of the Catholic school.'"

THE CATHOLIC SCHOOL ON THE THRESHOLD OF THE THIRD MILLENNIUM §9

---

1. In what moments or events in your own spiritual journey has Jesus Christ been a source of truth and inspiration? How can you continue to cultivate an ongoing relationship with Christ in your ministry as a Catholic school leader?

2. Recall a time when you were moved while praying over one of Jesus' actions as recorded in Scripture. Did the ministry of Jesus involve a movement of compassion, confrontation or conversion? Of healing or heartache? Of the miraculous or the mundane? How can you model a prayerful relationship with Christ for your school community?

3. What are the most effective ways your school promotes holistic development, including care for the head, the heart, and the soul? How is this development manifest for students? For parents? For administrators, teachers, and staff? For the school board?

PETER CORRIGAN

"The extent to which the Christian message is transmitted through education depends to a very great extent on the teachers. The integration of culture and faith is mediated by the other integration of faith and life in the person of the teacher."

THE CATHOLIC SCHOOL §43

Loving God,
I have looked for Your guidance in my vocation, and You have chosen me to serve You as a teacher. Be with me as I work to communicate Your love through my vocation.

Let my students look to me as a model of faith. Help me reflect Your love by the way I teach and communicate with my students.

You sent us Your Son as a perfect model for teachers. What can I learn from Christ the teacher? How can I incorporate His message into my craft?

Walk with me as I serve You through my vocation as a teacher.
Amen.

PATRICK FENNESSY

"Education in the faith by the parents should begin in the child's earliest years. This already happens when family members help one another to grow in faith by the witness of a Christian life in keeping with the Gospel. Family catechesis precedes, accompanies, and enriches other forms of instruction in the faith. Parents have the mission of teaching their children to pray and to discover their vocation as children of God. The parish is the Eucharistic community and the heart of the liturgical life of Christian families; it is a privileged place for the catechesis of children and parents."

CATECHISM OF THE CATHOLIC CHURCH §2226

---

*G*rowing up in a large Italian-Catholic family, I was very accustomed to praying as a family and going to church together. My parents were active parishioners leading the Youth group, volunteering for parish events and being members of the Knights of Columbus and PTA. As a result, my siblings and I were volunteers for numerous parish events. This active role came naturally to me and my parents always emphasized the importance of being active in the church and using my unique God-given talents to serve others.

Our parish involvement translated into our home life and we always prayed together before meals and before bed. The month of May was a special time of prayer in our household as we decorated a statue of Mary and said a rosary as a family each day. These traditions and others similar to it gave me a strong foundation for my prayer life.

Attending a Catholic school reinforced these values, and has helped me on my journey into becoming a faithful Catholic adult. Although I have faced challenges and had a few doubts, the foundation built by my parents and my parish family allowed me to find the answers and strengthen my relationship with God.

ANNE CHRISTINE BARBERA

"But let teachers recognize that the Catholic school depends upon them almost entirely for the accomplishment of its goals and programs."

GRAVISSIMUM EDUCATIONIS §8

Lord,
Being a teacher in a Catholic school is a tremendous opportunity. Students, parents, administrators, and colleagues depend upon me.

When I contribute to a team of educators, what we can accomplish is almost endless. Not only am I teaching my subject area or grade level, but I am teaching the faith.

Help me to identify, understand, and share in the goals of this school. Allow me to find the tools I need to contribute to the mission and vision of my school.

I have much to give to a world that needs Your light. Let me use Your Son as my example as a teacher to others. Thank You for this tremendous opportunity to serve You and Your community.
Amen.

DAN TULLY

"Teachers should understand that they are role models for their students in pursuing their intellectual and moral maturity."

PRINCIPLES FOR EDUCATIONAL REFORM IN THE UNITED STATES p. 6

---

1. In what ways do you engage in continuing education or continual improvement?

2. Describe the last thing you learned. How did you share that with your students? Other faculty and staff? Do you regularly incorporate new material, examples, or activities in your teaching?

3. What learning models do you find most effective for your own learning? How do you incorporate these in your classroom? Do you make any effort to try other learning models? How do you incorporate other learning models in your classroom?

4. How would you describe your relationship with and attitude toward the students, parents, faculty, and staff at your school? How would your students, parents, and your colleagues describe your relationship with them and other key stakeholders? Is there a disconnect between your view and that of others? If so, what changes can you make?

SISTER BARBARA KANE, O.P.

"The project of the Catholic school is convincing only if carried out by people who are deeply motivated, because they witness to a living encounter with Christ, in whom alone 'the mystery of man truly becomes clear.' These persons, therefore, acknowledge a personal and communal adherence with the Lord, assumed as the basis and constant reference of the inter-personal relationship and mutual cooperation between educator and student."

EDUCATING TOGETHER IN CATHOLIC SCHOOLS §4

J was a well-established teacher, having been at my school for almost six years, when I first heard about Mary. One of our kindergarten aides had left the year before under unclear circumstances. The staff was sad and a bit confused when she simply stopped coming. As we prepared for a new year, we heard rumors of the woman hired to be the new aide—Mary.

Mary was a middle-aged woman with no children of her own. Rumor had it that she had done some work with Catholic schools, but most of her experience was in public schools and with mostly middle-school students. How would she fit in this new role, especially working with some of our youngest students?

September quickly ran into October and November. We learned more about the real Mary. She had, in fact, worked extensively in Catholic schools. She left only after suggesting that her previous principal hire a less expensive, less experienced teacher to cover budgetary shortfalls. She was a deeply religious woman. She would go out of her way to make small treats for the staff including creative touches always accompanied with a Biblical reference reminding us of our purpose as Catholic educators. Her infectious laughter could be heard from one end of the building to the other. Her smile and positive attitude brought a real change to the attitudes of our staff.

Her effect on the students was even more powerful. She spent most of her time in an unconnected part of the building working with a few of our neediest students, yet whenever she came to the main building she was greeted with "Hello!" from students of all grade levels. They gave her small tokens of affection. She gave them her whole attention and then sent them on their way with a quick reference to God's love for them.

As the year finished, the staff came to the quiet understanding that Mary would be leaving us in June. The level of sadness was overwhelming. But as we all looked back over the year, it became abundantly clear that if ever there was a woman that reflected a living encounter with the presence of God, it was Mary.

HEATHER LINDSAY

"The educational process is not simply a human activity; it is a genuine Christian journey toward perfection."

THE RELIGIOUS DIMENSION OF EDUCATION IN A CATHOLIC SCHOOL §48

1. How can education help us attain perfection?

2. What does perfection look like in a classroom?

3. How can we incorporate elements of the Christian journey into the modern classroom?

RACHEL ROSEBERRY

"The implementation of a real educational community, built on the foundation of shared projected values, represents a serious task that must be carried out by the Catholic school. In this setting, the presence both of students and of teachers from different cultural and religious backgrounds requires an increased commitment of discernment and accompaniment."

EDUCATING TOGETHER IN CATHOLIC SCHOOLS §5

1. Often, Catholic schools are noted as being a community full of single-minded individuals only interested in their faith. The truth is that Catholic schools are vibrant communities full of men and women who are Catholics and non-Catholics, of different ethnicities and cultures, and who have a wide array of interests. Do you respond to differences in light of joining all together into a communion of life? How can you better use these cultural vibrancies to better motivate yourself and others to come to deepen their relationship with Christ through education?

2. The Lord created us not that we would all be alike but that we would all be unique and therefore able to learn from all that surrounds us. Do you strive to learn from the uniqueness of your students both inside and outside of the classroom? How can you take what you experience through each of your students and better yourself as a role model?

3. Education is a necessity both inside and outside of the classroom walls. How often do you discuss important topics like diversity with your colleagues? Do you seek to learn from them in order that you may grow in your faith and therefore, grow in your ability to impart knowledge to your students?

KEVIN KIMBERLY

"Here, too, instruction in religious truth and values is an integral part of the school program. It is not one more subject alongside the rest, but instead it is perceived and functions as the underlying reality in which the student's experiences of learning and living achieve their coherence and their deepest meaning."

TO TEACH AS JESUS DID §103

Too often when people talk about Catholic school identity they do so in a compartmentalized sort of way—they highlight specific courses, like religion or theology, or special events in the year, such as all-school Masses or mission trips. These activities and events certainly do communicate the priority of Catholic identity in our schools, but they do not encapsulate it entirely.

The reality is that nothing in a Catholic school is outside the purview or influence of our Catholic faith. In other words, everything that happens in the school is and is inspired by our Catholic identity. What a great worldview to impart to our students—a view of life and of living that sees no division between the most important tenets of our faith and the work and daily tasks of our vocation.

At the heart of this worldview is the powerful belief that, in our Catholic schools, there is "no separation between time for learning and time for formation." This is the true measure of our Catholic identity.

ANTHONY HOLTER

175

"Given the importance of the work done by Catholic educators, I join the Synod Fathers in gratefully encouraging all those devoted to teaching in Catholic schools—priests, consecrated men and women and committed lay people—'to persevere in their most important mission.'"

ECCLESIA IN AMERICA §71

Dear Lord,
As we begin each school year, new challenges will arise and test our dedication. Allow us as educators to be reminded that our vocation is not one for the weak or disheartened.

Help us to be courageous in our endeavors, pushing ourselves and our students to learn and grow in new ways.

We did not choose our path because of a fickle desire; You chose us to be Your followers, guiding those with whom we have been entrusted.

Renew in us our passion and zeal for knowledge so that our students gain a better appreciation for learning. Allow us to be strengthened in our mission that we may bring students closer to You.
Amen.

ANNE CHRISTINE BARBERA

"Parents have a particularly important part to play in the educating community, since it is to them that primary and natural responsibility for their children's education belongs. Unfortunately in our day there is a widespread tendency to delegate this unique role. Therefore it is necessary to foster initiatives which encourage commitment, but which provide at the same time the right sort of concrete support which the family needs and which involve it in the Catholic school's educational project."

THE CATHOLIC SCHOOL ON THE THRESHOLD OF THE THIRD MILLENNIUM §20

---

1. How can educators involve parents in the education of their children in ways that not only connect educators and parents, but children and parents?

2. What are ways to value parents' role in education so that they appreciate and take responsibility for their primary influence on their children?

3. How important is it to encourage family participation in the teaching of religious values and academic goals in Catholic education?

MELISSA REGAN

"The achievement of this specific aim of the Catholic school (teaching for the growth of the faith) depends not so much on subject matter or methodology as on the people who work there."

THE CATHOLIC SCHOOL §43

As superintendent, I am involved in the hiring and orientation of our new principals. One of the constant reminders that I offer these individuals is that the staff they have in their first year is the staff, for the most part, hired by the previous administrator. As they complete the evaluations of the staff, offer contracts for the following year and eventually sign the contracts they become a community of learners that they chose. What an awesome responsibility!

Whether the teachers were hired by the current administrator or the predecessor, it is the responsibility of the administrator to create an environment where the teacher can grow and realize the gifts he/she has to offer to the school community. In a Catholic school this is extremely important. Certainly we want the person to be knowledgeable in the subject area and to have appropriate knowledge for the age of the students. However, in a Catholic school, we also must be leaders of the faith community, helping each teacher recognize the ministry of teaching. Each teacher in a Catholic school must give witness to the values espoused in the mission statement of the Catholic school; we are called to teach and live these values. While some teachers may be of other faith traditions, they are part of the community that is committed to integrating the values of the Catholic faith in all that we do.

As leaders in a Catholic school, let us not forget the entire community. Invite the secretary, bookkeeper, custodian, and other staff members to attend the annual retreat and to pray together. All individuals, both in the classroom and outside of the classroom, are part of the faith community in which the students will receive their education.

SISTER MARY JANE HERB, IHM

"One specific characteristic of the educational profession assumes its most profound significance in the Catholic educator: the communication of truth. For the Catholic educator, whatever is true is a participation in Him who is the Truth; the communication of truth, therefore, as a professional activity, is thus fundamentally transformed into a unique participation in the prophetic mission of Christ, carried on through one's teaching."

LAY CATHOLICS IN SCHOOLS §16

Dear God,
You have given me the responsibility to discern Your truth.

Help me to better communicate this truth to my students, Your children that have been entrusted to my care.

Help me to shape their minds and help me to prepare them for a life in this world as well as life eternal.

Help me to always understand the importance of my vocation as a participant in Your mission on Earth.
Amen.

RACHEL ROSEBERRY

"The Church is deeply grateful to everyone dedicated to the educational mission in a Catholic school; it is confident that, with the help of God, many others will be called to join in this mission and will respond generously."

THE RELIGIOUS DIMENSION OF EDUCATION IN A CATHOLIC SCHOOL §114

I laugh along with the kids as she pulls out a large set of plastic hands and smashes them together to indicate that an exciting part of the story had begun. My eyes scan the room and I see twenty-two sets of eyes locked on her, awaiting the next segment of the story. Who knew that stories from the Old Testament could be so exciting?

My observation report should consist of one line. It should say, "She loves the kids and they love her." The love is sincere and they look forward to her class every day. She does not need a textbook or handouts. She only needs the Holy Bible, a few classroom prompts, and her personality to light the world on fire each day.

My thoughts are interrupted when we come to a happy point of the story and she pulls out her "applause" sign from under her classroom podium. I join the students in applauding and we all laugh a bit more.

Her part ends and she instructs the students to gather into groups to work on some reflection questions relevant to the story. She smiles at me, then travels around the room monitoring the students' work. More questions pop into my head. Why does our society not treat this master of her trade with more respect? As a matter of comparison, a fast food restaurant manager probably makes double her salary as a religious educator. What about attention and praise?

My questions are answered as I watch her interacting with her students. She wants nothing but forty-two minutes of uninterrupted time with her treasures and to be left alone by the confusion of what lies beyond her classroom door. She defines what we should all aspire to be as Catholic educators.

CHRISTOPHER BOTT

"It is not by chance that the first and original educational environment is that of the natural community of the family. Schools, in their turn, take their place beside the family as an educational space that is communitarian, organic and intentional and they sustain their educational commitment, according to a logic of assistance."

EDUCATING TOGETHER IN CATHOLIC SCHOOLS §12

Heavenly Father,
Let the families and our faculty come together in community. Open channels of communication that we may work toward one common goal: that of bringing children to love and serve You.

Allow our school to reinforce family traditions and values and compensate for any shortcomings, material or otherwise.

Open our hearts to accept all families and teach everyone, not only the students. Also open our hearts, dear Lord, that we may learn from the families in order to improve our services and relations.

Create an environment of sharing and support that our school and our families become one through our devotion to You.
Amen.

ANNE CHRISTINE BARBERA

References

Catholic Church. (1997). *Catechism of the Catholic Church* (2nd ed.). New York: Doubleday.

Congregation for Catholic Education. (1988). *The religious dimension of education in a Catholic school: Guidelines for reflection and renewal.* Washington, DC: United States Catholic Conference.

Congregation for Catholic Education. (1998). *The Catholic school on the threshold of the third millennium.* Boston: Pauline Books and Media.

Congregation for Catholic Education. (2002). *Consecrated persons and their mission in schools: Reflections and guidelines.* Rome: Libreria Editrice Vaticana.

Congregation for Catholic Education. (2008). *Educating together in Catholic schools: A shared mission between consecrated persons and the lay faithful.* London: Catholic Truth Society. (Original work published 2007)

Leo XIII. (1885). *Spectata fides* [On Christian education]. Retrieved July 16, 2010, from http://www.vatican.va/holy_father/leo_xiii/ encyclicals/documents/hf_l-xiii_enc_27111885_spectata-fides_en.html

Leo XIII. (1890). *Sapientiae christianae* [On Christians as citizens]. Retrieved July 16, 2010, from http://www.vatican.va/holy_ father/leo_xiii/encyclicals/documents/hf_l-xiii_enc_10011890_ sapientiae-christianae_en.html

National Conference of Catholic Bishops. (1972). *To teach as Jesus did: A pastoral message on Catholic education.* Washington, DC: United States Catholic Conference.

National Conference of Catholic Bishops. (1990). *In support of Catholic elementary and secondary schools.* Washington, DC: United States Catholic Conference.

National Conference of Catholic Bishops. (1999). *Our hearts were burning with us: A pastoral plan for adult faith formation in the United States.* Washington, DC: United States Catholic Conference.

John Paul II. (1979). *Catechesi tradendae* [On catechesis in our time]. Washington, DC: United States Catholic Conference.

John Paul II. (1981). *Familiaris consortio* [The role of the Christian family in the modern world]. Boston: St. Paul Editions.

John Paul II. (1994). *Gratissimam sane* [Letter to families]. Washington, DC: United States Catholic Conference.

John Paul II. (1999). *Ecclesia in America* [The Church in America]. Boston: Pauline Books and Media.

John XXIII. (1961). *Mater et magistra* [On Christianity and social progress]. Boston: St. Paul Editions.

Paul VI. (1975). *Evangelii nuntiandi* [On evangelization in the modern world]. Washington, DC: United States Catholic Conference.

Pius XI. (1929). *Divini ilius magistri* [On Christian education]. Retrieved July 16, 2010, from http://www.vatican.va/holy_father/pius_xi/encyclicals/documents/hf_p-xi_enc_31121929_divini-illius-magistri_en.html

Pontifical Council for Justice and Peace. (2004). *The compendium of the social doctrine of the church.* Washington, DC: United States Conference of Catholic Bishops.

Sacred Congregation for Catholic Education. (1977). *The Catholic school.* Washington, DC: United States Catholic Conference.

Sacred Congregation for Catholic Education. (1982). *Lay Catholics in schools: Witnesses to faith.* Boston: St. Paul Editions.

United States Catholic Conference. (1976). *Teach them! A statement of the Catholic bishops.* Washington, DC: Author.

United States Catholic Conference, Committee on Education. (1995). *Principles for educational reform in the United States.* Washington, DC: Author.

United States Conference of Catholic Bishops. (2005). *Renewing our commitment to Catholic elementary and secondary schools in the third millennium.* Washington, DC: Author.

Vatican Council II. (1965a). *Gaudium et spes* [On the Church in the modern world]. In A. Flannery (Ed.), *Vatican Council II: The conciliar and post conciliar documents* (pp. 903-1001). Northport, NY: Costello Publishing Company.

Vatican Council II. (1965b). *Gravissimum educationis* [Declaration on Christian education]. In A. Flannery (Ed.), *Vatican Council II: The conciliar and post conciliar documents* (pp. 725-737). Northport, NY: Costello Publishing Company.

Document Index

Catechesi Tradendae 17, 117
Catechism of the Catholic Church 7, 15, 169
Catholic School, The 3, 9, 23, 30, 32, 50, 55, 56, 60, 65, 70, 75, 78, 83, 98,
    102, 109, 121, 124, 131, 133, 143, 145, 152, 157, 162, 168, 178
Catholic School on the Threshold of the Third Millennium, The 10, 48, 52,
    57, 82, 87, 93, 106, 116, 120, 167, 177
Compendium of the Social Doctrine of the Church 40
Consecrated Persons and Their Mission in Schools 8, 24, 41, 80, 132

Divini Ilius Magistri 18, 51, 79, 89, 105, 122, 136

Ecclesia in America 25, 53, 176
Educating Together in Catholic Schools 5, 16, 22, 36, 47, 67, 76, 94, 101,
    113, 114, 125, 134, 155, 159, 172, 174, 181
Evangelii Nuntiandi 66, 100

Familiaris Consortio 44, 62, 135

Gaudium et Spes 35, 92
Gratissimam Sane 19, 27, 45, 73
Gravissimum Educationis 2, 29, 34, 61, 96, 112, 139, 158, 170

In Support of Catholic Elementary and Secondary Schools 123

Lay Catholics in Schools 4, 11, 14, 31, 42, 46, 54, 63, 68, 74, 84, 108, 111,
    115, 119, 128, 142, 144, 148, 154, 156, 160, 164, 166, 179

Mater et Magistra 77, 85

Our Hearts Were Burning Within Us 12

Principles for Educational Reform in the United States 97, 107, 141, 171

Religious Dimension of Education in a Catholic School, The 13, 20, 33, 59,
    69, 81, 86, 88, 91, 104, 127, 138, 146, 161, 173, 180
*Renewing our Commitment to Catholic Elementary and Secondary Schools
    in the Third Millennium* 43, 49, 64, 72, 95, 110, 118, 140, 163

Sapientiae Christianae 37
Spectata Fides 150

Teach Them! 6, 26, 38, 126, 130, 147, 151
To Teach As Jesus Did 21, 28, 39, 58, 71, 90, 99, 103, 129, 137, 149, 153,
    165, 175

Contributor Index

Asmar, Kathy 28, 42, 83

Barbera, Anne Christine 23, 52, 69, 85, 131, 140, 151, 156, 169, 176, 181
Bott, Christopher 20, 32, 39, 60, 86, 93, 98, 111, 116, 130, 155, 163, 180
Burleigh, Sister Anne Catherine 24, 36-37, 65, 106, 110, 119

Cassel, Laura 33, 48, 71, 97, 105, 115
Corrigan, Peter 9, 35, 62, 96-97, 128, 167

Dygert, Brother William 4, 8, 47, 90, 121, 146

Engel, Max 25, 38, 56, 84, 101, 123
Engelland-Spohn, Sorin 15, 50, 118, 150

Fennessy, Patrick 57, 67, 108-109, 127, 149, 168
Frabutt, Jim 3, 59, 76, 103, 107, 117, 153, 166

Herb, Sister Mary Jane 22, 53, 80, 126, 165, 178
Hjerpe, Christie 17, 91, 102-103, 141, 148, 158
Holter, Anthony 10, 30, 64, 94, 104, 122, 135, 175

Kane, Sister Barbara 5, 34, 63, 132, 152, 171
Ketchum, Jennifer 13, 31, 87, 145
Kimberly, Kevin 11, 44, 82, 138-139, 162, 174

Lindsay, Heather 19, 58-59, 89, 112-113, 142-143, 172-173
Lyons, Pamela 7, 45, 77, 133, 144, 160

Moreau, Lori 6-7, 66-67, 79, 95, 113, 143
Myers, Sister John Paul 16, 41, 75, 92, 100, 154

Nuzzi, Father Ronald 12, 43, 70, 114-115, 134, 164

Regan, Melissa 26-27, 49, 68-69, 129, 159, 177
Roseberry, Rachel 27, 51, 55, 139, 173, 179
Ryan, Michelle 14-15, 40-41, 78, 99, 147, 161

Smiley, Azure 18, 54-55, 73, 88, 124, 137

Tully, Dan 21, 46, 81, 125, 157, 170

Watson, Sarah 29, 37, 72
Whiting, Rosann 2-3, 61, 74, 109, 120-121, 136

About the Contributors

KATHY ASMAR, Teacher, Sacred Heart Catholic School, Hattiesburg, Mississippi

ANNE CHRISTINE BARBERA, Teacher, Alliance for Catholic Education (ACE), St. Rita Catholic School, Fort Worth, Texas

CHRISTOPHER BOTT, Principal, Catholic Central High School, Troy, New York

SISTER ANNE CATHERINE BURLEIGH, O.P., Principal, Mount de Sales Academy, Catonsville, Maryland

LAURA CASSEL, Teacher, Alliance for Catholic Education (ACE), Guadalupe Regional Middle School, Brownsville, Texas

PETER CORRIGAN, Director of Student Activities, Saint Ignatius College Prep, Chicago, Illinois

BROTHER WILLIAM DYGERT, C.S.C., Superintendent, Catholic Diocese of Peoria, Illinois

MAX ENGEL, Graduate Student, The Catholic University of America, Washington, DC

SORIN ENGELLAND-SPOHN, Teacher, St. Xavier High School, Louisville, Kentucky

PATRICK FENNESSY, Vice Principal, St. Joseph School, Seattle, Washington

JIM FRABUTT, Faculty, The Mary Ann Remick Leadership Program, University of Notre Dame, Notre Dame, Indiana

SISTER MARY JANE HERB, I.H.M., Superintendent, Catholic Diocese of Albany, New York

CHRISTIE HJERPE, Teacher, Alliance for Catholic Education (ACE), Santa Cruz Catholic School, Tucson, Arizona

ANTHONY HOLTER, Faculty, The Mary Ann Remick Leadership Program, University of Notre Dame, Notre Dame, Indiana

SISTER BARBARA KANE, O.P., Principal, Dominican Academy, New York, New York

JENNIFER KETCHUM, Principal, St. Peter's Interparish School, Washington, DC

KEVIN KIMBERLY, Student, University of Notre Dame, Notre Dame, Indiana

HEATHER LINDSAY, Teacher, St. Paul School, Wellesley, Massachusetts

PAMELA LYONS, Principal, Assumption School, San Leandro, California

LORI MOREAU, Principal, Father Anglim Academy, Fort Myers, Florida

SISTER JOHN PAUL MYERS, O.P., Teacher and Religion Department Chair, St. Cecilia Academy, Nashville, Tennessee

FATHER RONALD NUZZI, Director, The Mary Ann Remick Leadership Program, University of Notre Dame, Notre Dame, Indiana

MELISSA REGAN, Student, University of Notre Dame, Notre Dame, Indiana

RACHEL ROSEBERRY, Student, University of Notre Dame, Notre Dame, Indiana

MICHELLE RYAN, Consultant, Dicoese of Arlington, Virginia

AZURE DEE SMILEY, Assistant Professor, University of Indianapolis, Indianapolis, Indiana

DAN TULLY, Principal, Notre Dame College Prep, Niles, Illinois

SARAH WATSON, Faculty, St. Xavier High School, Louisville, Kentucky

ROSANN WHITING, President, Ursuline Academy, Dedham, Massachusetts